SCOTTO SUNDAY SUPPERS *and* OTHER FABULOUS FEASTS

THE *Scotto Family*

ReganBooks

REGANBOOKS

AN IMPRINT OF HARPERCOLLINS PUBLISHERS

SCOTTO SUNDAY SUPPERS

and

OTHER FABULOUS FEASTS

Creative Entertaining for Every Occasion

A special thanks to

To Executive Chef Steve Santoro and Pastry Chef Chris Smreker: Thank you for your endless energy, creativity, and consistent originality.

To Raul Ramirez, our sous chef: Thank you for your hard work, diligence, and good spirit and for always being there for us. You made the photo shoots and recipe testing an enjoyable experience.

To Kerrie O'Brien, our sommelier: Thank you for keeping our spirits high and making our customers happy. We appreciate your hard work and knowledge of fine wines. You made wine pairing a breeze.

To our management team, Attilio Vosilla, James Rotunno, Rachel Novack, Johanna Madoff, and Patricia Herrera: Thank you for your support, hard work, and loyalty.

To Natasha Gelman, our bookkeeper, who has been with us since day one: Thank you for your commitment and perfection.

To Dennis Ryan, who has been with us since the day we opened: Thank you for your endless hours on the computer and your dedication to our customers.

To the rest of our staff: Thank you for your loyalty and perseverance.

And finally, to our loyal customers. We thank you for making us a part of your family.

❧

FIRST EDITION

Photography by QUENTIN BACON *Art direction by* MICHELLE ISHAY
Designed by JUDITH STAGNITTO ABBATE / ABBATE DESIGN

Printed on acid-free paper

Library of Congress Cataloging-in-Publication Data

Scotto Sunday suppers and other fabulous feasts : creative entertaining for every occasion / the Scotto Family.—1st ed.
  p.cm.
  Includes index.
  ISBN 0-06-081563-9
  1. Cookery, Italian. 2. Entertaining. I. Scotto, Marion. II. Fresco by Scotto (Restaurant)
  TX723.S3674 2005
  642'.4—dc22   2005046265

05 06 07 08 09 IM 10 9 8 7 6 5 4 3 2 1

Thank you to our colleagues for their kindness
and support throughout the years:

— ❧ —

Cindy Adams
Betsy Alexander
Gerette Allegra
Michael Bass
Jason Binn
Frank Bruni
Jim Clayton
Larry Cohn
Katie Couric
Ann Curry
Andrea D'Ambrosio
Tony Danza
Gillian Duffy
Florence Fabricant
Bobby Flay

Bill Geddie
Kathie Lee Gifford
Rudolph Giuliani
Gael Greene
Lisa Gregorich-Dempsey
John Grisham
Joan Hamburg
Richard Johnson
Bob Lape
Matt Lauer
Scott Matthews
Jason Oliver North
Rosie O'Donnell
Regis and Joy Philbin
Tony Potts
Robin Raisfel

Judith Regan
Ruth Reichl
Kelly Ripa
Al Roker
Amy Rosenblum
Hal Rubenstein
Sly Stallone
Linda Stasi
George Steinbrenner
Phil Suarez
Jonathan Tisch
Donald Trump
Cheryl Wells
Bernie Young
Nina and Tim Zagat
Caryn and Jeff Zucker

This book is dedicated to

— ❧ —

Judith Regan:

We thank you for your guidance, encouragement, and support.
You made our cookbook experiences a gourmet holiday.

Jeff Zucker:

Our gratitude and respect for all that you have done for us.
You made us what we are today; we couldn't have done it without you!

Contents

For most Italian-Americans there is only one day that counts. It's Sunday—the one day that the whole family gathers at Mom's house for dinner at three in the afternoon. It's not that we're not sophisticated enough to wait for the more fashionable eight o'clock, it's just that there are so many courses that the kids might not get to school on time the next day if we started at eight!

Failure to show up for Sunday dinner, as most Italians know, is no big deal—especially if you don't care about being excommunicated from the clan or breaking your mother's heart. This heart condition, incidentally, affects Italian mothers of all ages, and appears within minutes of the first pregnancy.

Sunday dinner is *all* about the food and not *only* about the food at the same time. Sunday family dinner focuses on what the food conveys—love, safety, warmth, hilarity, solidarity, and sometimes high-wire emotions. All that stuff from a meatball? You bet.

It begins when you wake up to the smell, *that* smell, of onions and garlic frying in the kitchen on Sunday morning because someone got up first to start the sauce.

Sunday dinner is about getting together to fight for space at the stove, it's about the little ones learning to make meatballs, and the big ones coming home from church to sneak a little *bagno da*. (Pronounced *bon*-yo dah, it literally means, "to bathe" or "I wet." In other words, to dip that chunk of Italian bread you swiped into the sauce pot for a little taste!) Yes, there *is* a word for it. In fact, there's an Italian word for everything related to food—with the possible exception of "single serving."

—THE SCOTTO FAMILY

THAT WAS THEN: MARION

Ahhhh, the smell of Sunday. For some, it's the pungent odor of incense in church; for others, it might be the new car smell they remember from those old-fashioned Sunday drives with their parents. For me, the aroma of meatballs frying in the kitchen has always meant not only "Sunday" but "home."

I grew up in South Brooklyn in a brownstone shared by three families—and not strangers' families, *family* families (my extended family). Each floor had its own mother at the helm and its own special Sunday smell.

Aunt Mary's floor smelled sweet. She hailed from Bari, where they sweeten their meatballs with raisins! Aunt Jo's floor smelled serious. She made her sauce with pork—and there was no mistaking that particularly de-

licious aroma. Of course, to my mind, our floor smelled best because my mother Rose's sauce was the best. Was it because she combined pork *and* beef, or was it just because she was my mother?

In case you missed it, I've just given you a shortened version of what all Italians know by the time they're old enough to make it down the stairs into the kitchen by themselves: sauce is not just sauce! Every region has its own particular version of the Sunday staple, and each one is glorious in and of itself. Think of it as a red, tasty roadmap of Italy.

While I was growing up, Sunday was a day devoted to *eating*. And it still is. I think I've instilled in my own brood the same love of Sunday family dinners that I remember.

Back then the gatherings were always enormous—and actually, they still are. We were always at least twenty because whatever cousins were around would be sure to show up, too. I remember that while the women were busy in the kitchen, my dad and Uncle Joe, who were from Calabria, would practice their English in the living room. If you've ever been to Calabria, you know that the Calabrese dialect is to Italian what a deep Southern drawl is to the king's English.

Speaking Italian—in whatever dialect—was strictly forbidden on Sundays; they were there to practice their English. For them, the pressure to fit in, to become "un Americano," was great. While I understand it, it remains one tradition I *don't* treasure, because I still don't speak fluent Italian. But the men were *adamant* about speaking English on Sundays—and it was always fun to listen to them practicing by reading the *Daily News* aloud to one another.

I especially remember going into uncontrolled gales of laughter when one of them would announce to the other, "Maxwell have a cuppa coffee." This actually meant, "May as well have a cup of coffee." Funny as it was, it became a sensitive issue after my daughter Rosanna was born and she began speaking broken English as a toddler.

But there was no confusion over American versus Italian when it came to the food. Dinner started at three in the afternoon back then, and it still does today.

The first dish—of course—was antipasto. That meant salami; proscuitto; gorgeous, *delizioso* Parmigiano; and hunks of bread—whatever hadn't already been swiped earlier for dipping in the sauce, that is. Then we moved on to the pasta in the Sunday sauce, which we called "gravy" because the sauce was made with meat as well as tomatoes. The meats that had been simmering in the gravy became the next course. These gravy meats were never served with the pasta. There could be any combination of meats in there—from sausage, spinelli, or pork chops, to meatballs or bracciole (which literally translated means armrests, probably because the rolled meat

looks a bit like an armrest). But that wasn't all. Baked chicken or sausage, and sometimes both, generally followed those courses!

We always finished off with an assortment of Italian cheeses and pastries. Strangely enough, no one was especially overweight—not in the way Americans routinely are in this day and age—although there was always the fear that one of us wasn't quite full!

On the off chance that someone might *still* be hungry, all of the gravy meat was kept out after supper so everyone could pick. After all, the men could work up quite an appetite playing gin rummy, and so could the women practicing the cha cha to Xavier Cugat records in the living room.

I remember how exhausted my mother usually was after this feeding orgy every week. I didn't understand it until I had a family and a kitchen of my own. Back then women did all the cooking *and* all the cleaning up. There were no dishwashers—not of the mechanical or of the male kind. Needless to say, the men never lifted a finger—unless it was to pick up a card!

Today, while things have changed, much remains the same. My kids claim that when they were growing up "the women's work" became "the kids' work," at least as far as serving and cleaning up went. Rosanna says, "We were cheap labor!" Trust me, she exaggerates.

I tell them that if they hadn't learned early, they wouldn't be the great restaurateurs they are today. Together we've created something we treasure as much as our Scotto Sundays.

The more things change, the more they change only slightly—for us, anyway. Sunday dinner was then and is still the highlight of the week for our family—no matter how busy we are with our New York City lives.

Our family has grown over the years to what some might consider an alarming size! At least for dinner. There are eighteen regulars, including eight grandkids, before the friends even *begin* to show up.

Nowadays, however, the men not only help out, they are as much a part of the whole process—cooking, preparing, and entertaining—as the women are. (After all, the excuse about needing to practice their English by reading the papers out loud on Sundays just doesn't cut the *sopressata* anymore, since we're into our third generation of Americans.)

At any rate, the men had *better* lend a hand, because sometimes, on a summer Sunday, we'll lay out an outdoor table at our Southampton house for forty people!

Sure, we tried being apart on Sundays for a while, but it just didn't work. Rosanna and her husband, Lou, even had a house upstate where "it would be just us and the kids and we'd hang out with Mr. and Mrs. Squirrel." Nice, but where was the rest of the family?

As our parents' house was being built in Southampton, we all kept saying how much we missed being together for Sunday dinner. Finally Elaina said what we were all secretly thinking anyway: "Let's build together." And we did. We're one very big, happy family in one very big, happy house.

Not that it's ever just us for Sunday dinner, mind you. Heck, on any given Sunday it's usually an assortment of family and friends and their kids. Only one rule applies: Wear something loose, preferably with an elastic waistband. You'll need it.

We learned a long time ago that it's not just about the food, no matter how much of it there is. It's about the whole experience of a good, old-fashioned Italian Sun-

day dinner—from the giant outdoor table covered in fresh flowers and candles, to the colorful china, to the beautiful linens in great colors, and finally to the dinner itself—the one that begins with antipasto and ends with cheese and dessert.

During it all, there is always lots and lots of music. It's the background of our lives, whether it's Mom's insane karaoke machine (which has given us too, too many laughs), or tunes played by local musicians. It's not Sunday without music to sing, dance, and eat along with!

Each Sunday dinner begins with our own version of mimosas—champagne and blood orange juice mixed together. During cocktails we bring out our homemade margherita pizzas with mozzarella, ripe tomatoes, and fresh-picked basil, and then it's on to our homemade potato and zucchini chips smothered in melted Gorgonzola cheese.

Still hungry? How about a little imported prosciutto, sopressata, a bit of tangy Parmesan, some grilled eggplant and peppers, wrapped around a homemade bread stick or eaten alone or with a piece of cheese bread?

That's for starters.

Then of course comes the Sunday sauce and pasta course. Funny, but when we first opened our restaurant, Fresco by Scotto, we didn't even have Sunday sauce on the menu. It's something we grew up with and didn't consider "restaurant food,"—just our own homey comfort food. We thought it was, well, maybe a little pedestrian for our patrons. Right? Wrong!

Our friends demanded it, and now Sunday Sauce is as much a staple at Fresco as it is on the Sunday Scotto table.

Speaking of sauce, remember how Mom said she felt that her mom's Sunday sauce was best way back when? Well, we kids feel the same way about *our* mom's sauce now, although now we have to amend it these days to "our *parents'* sauce" because our dad has become the chief Sunday sauce maker at our house.

The sauce, by the way, is always prepared way ahead of time (as is most of the food, or we wouldn't have time to enjoy our guests *or* ourselves!), so that by the time we're ready to serve it, it's just a matter of boiling the "macaroni" and then tossing it with the sauce.

Done? Are you serious? After the pasta course comes the *third* course—just like in the old days—the gravy meat, which we love to bring out on gorgeous, gigantic platters, encouraging everyone to grab their forks and dig right in! *Mangia!*

The final course? Cheese, fruit, and usually something dangerously fattening and fantastically sweet, topped off with lots of espresso and a selection of after-dinner drinks.

But hey, don't think we aren't open and even willing to change our ways from time to time, even on Sundays. In fact, on lazy Sundays, we love nothing better than to grill up some juicy porterhouse steaks—a task that usually falls to Rosanna's husband Lou and Elaina's husband Dan (who even got a branding iron last Christmas). How's that for change?

But change isn't *always* good. Take that one Sunday when we somehow invited too many people (including another professional restaurateur). There were just too many steaks for Dan and Lou to handle, so we talked about hiring a local "professional" grill man—a barbecuing expert. (Yes, you *can* find someone to do anything in the Hamptons.)

Admittedly, Mom did not, repeat did *not*, like the whole idea at all. But we finally beat her down and *forced* her to hire the BBQ guy. And really, everything was going great. Well, until we noticed that giant flames were shooting into the sky from our grill, otherwise known as the Towering Inferno BBQ!

The professional grill guy looked more like Fire Marshall Bill than the pro he claimed to be, what with those flames shooting up behind him! And those eighteen formerly gorgeous Porterhouse steaks we'd bought? Suffice it to say that even the dog ran away in disgust.

So much for bringing in outsiders. But as every Italian grandmother likes to say, "everything happens for a reason," and we learned two very valuable lessons from the flaming chef that day. Number 1: Keep the marinade away from any guy who thinks steak sauce is a food group. Number 2: Always have more food—much more—than you need.

Needless to say, we went back to cooking for ourselves. So yes, it's true, the more things change, the more they change only slightly—for us, anyway. That's especially true when it comes to Sunday dinners and to family.

Sure, we consider ourselves modern, sophisticated hosts, but hosts who also believe that there's still no place like home, where the smell of simmering sauce *is still* the smell of Sunday. The smell of home.

On Sunday *everybody* wants to be Italian. And why not? Our family, at least, keeps to the old traditions. We wish in a way that the Blue Laws were never rescinded and we simply couldn't go shoe shopping on Sundays. Instead we just pretend that everything is still closed and the family has to spend the day enjoying each other instead of crawling the malls.

Try it sometime—you might like it as much as we do. Think about it for a minute, would you rather sit down with twenty of your favorite friends and relatives, eat delicious food, talk politics, drink some wonderful wine, dish the dirt, eat some more superb food, argue some more about current events, and drink some even better wine (it gets better as the day goes on, somehow), or, say, spend the day buying tires? Hint: for us, *Never on Sunday* isn't just an old movie, it's a way of life. Well, "never and always," we should say: never mall crawl, always celebrate the day with loved ones.

Getting Sunday dinner out for the hordes may seem like a lot of work, but once you know the tricks of the trade, it's an easy labor of love. Here, then are our favorite hints, tips, and tricks for making Sundays simple, beginning with setting a super supper table.

You'd never think of going outside in curlers and a robe, would you? No, of course not, yet plenty of people who love to cook don't think beyond the food. They end up serving their gorgeous food on a table that looks like an unmade bed!

Not to pick on anyone in particular, but have you noticed that many men, even men who *love* to cook think that the meal prep is done if the food gets to the table in one piece and on time? Wrong!

Meals should be a feast for all the senses, beginning with the sight of the Sunday table. Setting the table sets the mood. For us that means pretty linens, fresh flowers (this is nonnegotiable, by the way!), and seasonal decorations. By "seasonal" we mean anything from the arts

and crafts projects the kids made that week in school, to tiny pumpkins fresh off the stands set at each place setting, to giant bunches of eucalyptus bought fresh at the farm stand (which can last for weeks).

In summer, only God and Mom usually have any clear idea of how many people will show up at our Southampton backyard for midafternoon dinner, so we try to keep it easy—and big.

We have four four-by-eight foot tables that we put together to form one loooong table. The key here is having that four-foot width so that there's plenty of room to fit all of the delicious antipasto that we've preplated for our guests.

No, you don't need to spend thousands to make your table look like a million bucks. Have you thought about burlap linen? It's cheap, chic, fun, and nobody's going to get sent to the kid's table if they spill wine all over it. (Actually there is no kid's table at our house. Since kids are people too, they learn table manners early and often!)

If you're not in the mood to sew up the hems on all that burlap linen (and really, who is?), you can always fray all the edges for a casual, crazy summer look. This, mind you, is a great project for the kids and will keep them busy for, well, years.

Think placemats. Our favorite summer table (er, tables) is covered in burlap with colorful placemats with matching napkins over it, in all kinds of great colors. They're pretty, they're washable, and they're perfect for the outdoors.

In summer we also love sunflowers—in pots, pitchers, and vases. Sunshine for the table!

As for the food, the table is filled by the time the guests arrive with platters of tomato, basil, mozzarella—the tomatoes are so great in summer that we use them in every dish we can—sopressata, and Parmesan. We fill some pitchers with extra-tall bread sticks and others with red or white wine infused with peaches that we slice into the wine hours beforehand.

But make no mistake about it—all the great food in the world does not alone guarantee a great Sunday

dinner party. The two key ingredients to any memorable Sunday supper are the guests, and their proximity to the action, i.e. the kitchen!

Our rule about guests is there is no rule. If it's family and close friends, it's every man, woman, and child for themselves as far as seating goes. If it's a bigger, more unwieldy group, we try to figure out beforehand just which guests would enjoy sitting next to one another. It's always fun to mix it up, and have, say, the local politician next to the town's gossip columnist!

At the end of the day, however (or more accurately, at the beginning of the dinner), success comes down to the timing. We always try to precook as much food as is humanly possible, although not all of it, of course, can be done that way.

But in reality dinner isn't dinner and Sunday isn't Sunday unless everyone makes his or her way at least once into the kitchen. The Italian kitchen on Sunday is where the party begins, where the socializing starts. We always joke that we should have just done away with the living room and tripled the size of the kitchen! Anyway, you'd need a nose transplant if you could resist the smells coming out of our Sunday kitchen—especially the pungent aroma of Gorgonzola cheese bubbling over the tops of our potato and zucchini chips (also known as 'zola spuds and zukes).

The kitchen is to Italian Sunday as smoke is to flame, romance is to love, and marble is to sculpture. It's the place where it begins—and the place everyone wants to be—the place where it's all created.

aybe it's because we're brought up with wine at dinner (most Italian kids are allowed a tiny cup of way-watered-down wine with Sunday dinner) but for Italian-Americans, wine is an easy, natural part of our lives. It can be for you, too.

Sure, the key to a great Sunday dinner (or any dinner) is pairing the right wine with great food, but figuring out what wines to serve should be part of the fun of preparing the meal, not an intimidating experience.

We've all heard the scary admonitions about (God forbid!) serving a red wine with fish, or a white wine with steak. Who makes this stuff up, anyway? We find that people will tackle the most complicated recipe before they presume to figure out what wine to pair with that complicated dish. Why? Believe it when we tell you that you don't have to take a course in wines to figure out how to pair wines with food.

Just like our Sunday suppers, we like to keep things simple, yet refined. It's not about rules, but more about what type of wine suits your style, as well as what wine will complement the flavor of the dish you're serving.

While there are no hard and fast rules at a Scotto Sunday supper, we do follow a few simple guidelines. First, think "body." No, not your own (it's Sunday, relax!), but the body of the wine in relation to the "body" of the food (see the next section for details). A light, crisp, pinot grigio, for example, would be lost with a pan-roasted wild king salmon. We'd serve that fish with, say, a pinot noir.

On the other hand, if you're serving a poached fillet of sole, you don't want a full-bodied wine to overwhelm the subtlety of the fish. In that case, you might think about a Riesling.

Take into account how the preparation of the food works with the type of wine you'll serve. Cold foods such as seafood ceviches, salads, and vegetable antipasti should be matched with acidic wines such as sauvignon blanc, pinto grigio, and Arneis.

Grilled foods? Think spicy, think cedary, think syrah, zinfandel, and cabernet. When it's fish you're grilling, the one secret to a perfect pairing is to simply remember that the oilier the fish, the "bigger" the wine should be. So, if you're preparing grilled tuna, for instance, pair it with a heavy Napa Valley chardonnay. If it's grilled trout, then think Sonoma chardonnay, which is a lighter wine. The main thing to remember is that you don't want the wine to overpower the food and you don't want the food to overpower the wine.

Believe it or not, the same thing goes for dessert. Here, too, there's only *one* rule: dessert wines *must* be sweeter than the dessert you're serving, or your wine will hit the palate like last week's diet soda. Pair the Buttermilk Panna Cotta with Fresh Spring Berries with Freemark Abby Edelwein Gold 1999. A sweeter dessert,

such as Peach Upside Down Cake, goes well with Chateau Rieussec Sauternes 1999. Chocolate desserts, like the Bittersweet Chocolate Pudding Cake, can be paired with Les Clos de Pauilles Banyuls 2002.

BODY BEAUTIFUL

How exactly do you tell the "body" of a wine? It's logical: the first, best, and easiest way is color. A light-colored wine will naturally be less full-bodied than a darker-colored wine. For example, a straw-colored white wine like sauvignon blanc will be less full-bodied than a darker, golden, amber-colored chardonnay. Similarly, lighter colored red wines (dolcetto, pinot noir) will be less full-bodied than a blackberry-colored, opaque wine such as a syrah or cabernet.

Got it? Good. Another easy way to judge a wine's body is to check its viscosity (thickness). A simple way to do this is to pour a bit into a glass and swirl it around gently. How quickly or slowly does the wine flow back down the side of the glass? A light-bodied wine will move quickly and will not coat the glass the way a slower-moving full-bodied wine will. It's kind of like how you can tell the difference between heavy cream, whole milk, and skim milk.

Another way to know the body of a wine is to check the alcohol content. The higher the alcohol content, the more full-bodied the wine. Reds generally have more alcohol (for example, zinfandel, cabernet, and petit syrah). Slightly sweet wines (Riesling, Cali Chenin Blanc, gewürztraminers) are less potent because fermentation is stopped earlier to retain the residual sugar.

Then there's the matter of tannins (which help give wine depth of color as well as body). Tannins come from the skin, seeds, and stems of grapes as well as from the oak barrels. Red wines usually have more tannins be-cause there is more contact with the grape skins. Red wines are also subject to longer barrel aging than white wines.

When a white wine is exposed to oak, it will have a richer, creamier mouth feel, which boosts the perception of body in the wine. Usually only fuller-bodied white varietals (chardonnay) are aged in oak, otherwise the delicate nature of their varietal character would be overwhelmed (such as Reisling). Furthermore, when wines are aged *or* fermented in oak (*or both*), they will have a more "oaky" characteristic.

Now that wasn't so intimidating, was it?

Nothing is worse than waking up the day after a night with a good or a great wine to find that your head wants to leave home. Hey, how did that happen when that wine cost more than your engagement ring? The last thing you want to do is give your Sunday *guests* something more than a nice memory on Monday morning. You want them to remember the wine, not the whine!

Since the generally accepted idea is the cheaper the vino, the worse the sulfites, and the more expensive the wine, the fewer the sulfites, your guests may think you served a 59-cent wine in a 59-dollar bottle if they get a hangover headache.

Is it true that cheap wine has more sulfites? Sometimes. The truth is that *all* wines have sulfites, which are a naturally occurring by-product of fermentation. Yes, some winemakers do in fact add small amounts of sulfites as preservatives, but the latest research shows that "wine headaches" may not be so much the fault of sulfites as a person's tolerance to wine. It may be about how a person actually metabolizes wine. Sulfites are not only found in wine, but also in fruit juice, other kinds of beverages, and even in shrimp and pizza dough! When was the last time you ever heard somebody say, "Oh my aching head! I had too much shrimp last night!" There are no such things—yet, anyway—as twelve-step programs for pizzaholics, either!

That being said, it is true that people seem to have more trouble with red wine than white and with higher alcohol-content wines than lower. Again that may be because red wines typically have a higher alcohol content than whites.

California cabernets and zinfandels can have an alcohol content up to 15 percent, which borders on the alcohol content of fortified wine (wine that's been strengthened with brandy and/or herbs, roots, spices, and peels).

Right now, the most food-friendly and headache-avoiding wines for the sensitive are the white meritages from California, which are based on French varietals like Marsanne, Roussane, and Viognier. *Delizioso!* Or should we say, "*délicieux!*"

All that being said, in summer when it just seems too hot for wine, we love serving huge carafes of wine infused with peaches, or our own homemade sangria.

Wine shouldn't be a chore—it should be an enjoyment.

For a delicious, simple sangria, just fill a large pitcher with an inexpensive red or white wine and add cut up peaches, apples, oranges, and Cointreau or Grand Marnier to sweeten. Marinate in the fridge, and take it out fifteen minutes before serving. Make up a batch of kids' sangria using grape juice instead of wine.

Remember, it's not only the food and wine that makes the meal, it's also the company.

*D*oes it ever seem as though cooking that big Sunday dinner is easier than serving that big Sunday dinner? Well, take heart—you're not alone, because, frankly, it is. Maybe that's because in general, cooking the meal is always more fun than getting the meal to the table.

But what it shouldn't be is more stressful—although somehow it usually is. Why? Because unless you're in the biz—and are used to serving lots and lots of people every night—it can be a bit overwhelming to get all of that food onto all of those plates without breaking, spilling, or serving the pasta piping cold!

So how do you turn food for a crowd into a crowd-pleaser? Obviously, in a restaurant, the mechanics of getting the food to the table is part of the restaurant routine. The chefs prepare, the cooks plate the meals, and the wait staff brings the beautifully arranged plates to each diner.

Clearly, this isn't the routine in most family dinners at home, but you can learn to handle it as efficiently and with as much care with a few tricks of the trade.

Here's our routine.

When we have more than twenty people, we mirror the platters across each other so the meat on one end will match the meat on the other. This eliminates the dreaded buffet line. People are over for dinner—not a fundraiser—and they shouldn't be standing around waiting to get fed.

When it's a casual Sunday dinner, we wrap each place setting in a napkin and put them in a beautiful, lined basket on the buffet.

In the center of the buffet table itself? A gorgeous three-foot-tall silver vase filled to overflowing with extra-tall Casablanca lilies that are not only beautiful, but wonderfully fragrant.

BUFFING UP THE BUFFET

If there are several different choices (and legend has it that one Sunday in March of 1959, there weren't enough choices at a Scotto Sunday dinner), we usually set up a beautiful buffet right in our kitchen.

We use the large island in the middle of our kitchen to actually set out the food—the wine and the glasses are already set out on the dining table. There is nothing worse than people trying to carry a plate with one hand and a wine glass in the other. The platters we use are enormous and weigh six tons apiece. This is practical as well as smart, because not only do they hold a lot, but they don't shift and sway, which can cause accidents. We arrange the platters on the island by courses so as people go along, they can fill their plates in the logical progression—salads, pasta, veggies, meat, and fish.

SIT DOWN AND TALK UP!

When the occasion calls for a more elegant dinner, we do "platter-and-pass," and we break down each item in several platters—never more than six portions on a platter.

Now, of course whether you're serving meat or pasta, there's always the possibility of a lot of nasty spills. It's not the tablecloths we worry about, it's our guests' clothes! So we try really hard to keep the liquids on the platters to a minimum. You can always pass the sauce and gravies separately.

Look for platters that are lightweight and simple in design. The lightness makes for easy passing, and the simplicity of design won't conflict with the carefully and beautifully arranged food. Once the first round of food is passed, we condense the platters and place them smack in the center of the table.

If it's a very special event or a super-elegant party, we always go with a plated meal. We usually start before guests arrive by making up the plates with homemade mozzarella, vine-ripened tomatoes, and maybe some grilled eggplant, or a little eggplant salad.

We make 'em up and line 'em up—that way when it's time to serve, all we have to do is drizzle some extra-virgin olive oil and some aged balsamic vinegar and the first course is completed!

Since we've done most of the cooking before the guests arrive—we've prepped the salads, marinated the meat and the fish, and of course, made the sauce for the pasta—it takes only ten minutes to cook the pasta and another ten if there is grilling to be done.

We all have a job. Ro and Elaina are in charge of salads and appetizers, Mom and Dad take care of the pasta, and Anthony and John are the grill men. One of us is always in charge of plating, another wipes down the sides of plates (drips, spills, and so on), and two of us are the servers.

This might seem obvious, but just make sure there is salt, pepper, red pepper, and cheese on the table. The last thing you want to do is to stop the flow while you run to get seasonings for a guest.

If we are plating desserts, we usually do two different types and serve every other person the same dessert. If not, we simply put all the cakes in the center of the table and serve from there.

It's actually a lot simpler once you realize that dinners that go well, flow well.

*H*ave you ever been to a dinner party with great food and good people in a nice house, and it *still* felt like torture? What happened? Or better yet, *how* did it happen?

Short of inviting a newly separated couple and the husband's new, er, side dish, or the wife's new boy toy, you *can* avoid having a bad dinner party. This is especially true on Sundays, when everybody should just be calm, relaxed, and open to enjoying food, wine, and each other.

We Scottos have been studying Sunday suppers for a looong time, as you know. What always works? What never works? And how can you know for sure? We can't tell you *whom* to invite, but we can tell you some of our favorite tips and tricks for not only avoiding disaster, but creating dinners that everyone will remember. In a good way!

> ### MAKING YOUR GUESTS
> ### FEEL WELCOME

A FEW DAYS BEFORE

- Fill your salt and pepper shakers, count your linens, make sure your platters and glasses are sparkling, and polish the silver. Think about table favors and how you'll set your table.

- Make sure your table linens are clean, pressed, and ready to do service.

- Buy beautiful, disposable hand towels for all guest bathrooms. They come in linen-like paper now and are great to stack in little baskets next to the sink. Be sure, too, that clean terry hand towels are ready for the guest bathrooms as well.

- Think about the flowers. Is there a farmer's market in your town on Saturdays where you can buy whatever is freshest for Sunday's table?

- Label the platters. Even though we like to think we already know everything there is to know, we did learn a *great* trick from our appearances on cooking segments for *Today*. Did you ever think of labeling your platters in advance? This not only saves you the stress of scrambling around at the last minute looking for the right platter for the right food, but it keeps everything flowing easily. It would be a terrible thing to have to put that beautiful bunch of steamed lobsters right on your guests' laps because you couldn't find the right platter at the crucial moment!

- When you plan the menu, be sure to choose food combinations you can both physically prepare and heat up at the same time, given the oven and stove space available in your kitchen.

JUST BEFORE THE GUESTS ARRIVE

- Finish making and arranging all the cold appetizers so that they're ready to serve as soon as you hear the first doorbell chime.

- Stationary snacks should be placed where they are accessible without being easily knocked over.

- Set up the bar—and that means wherever it is that you'll keep the liquor and prepare the drinks.

- Hors d'oeuvres should be cooked, hot, and ready to be passed.

- Post a menu and timetable in your kitchen so that you don't forget a salad in the refrigerator or a vegetable in the oven. Our friend Linda Stasi says it's a Sunday family tradition at her house to *always* forget the bread in the oven until it starts to smoke up the entire house.

- Be sure to pick out the music and have it playing on the stereo before guests arrive. It's fun to burn your own CDs with a mix of your favorite music so you don't have to think about it once the dinner gets started. Our new favorites are the Rod Stewart standards album, Stevie Wonder's *Greatest Hits*, and Regis and Joy Philbin's *When You're Smiling*.

LITTLE THINGS TO REMEMBER

GOD IS IN THE DETAILS

- Even if you're richer than a Trump, *you* should always be waiting for your guests, ready to greet them with a great big smile. Marion remembers going to a big dinner party once, and the staff was there to greet the guests—but the hosts weren't. They didn't deign to join their own guests for more than half an hour. It made everyone feel very uncomfortable. What were they doing, getting fancied up? Trust us, no amount of lipstick is that important!

- Introduce your guests to one another during cocktails, giving them a tiny bit of info (when appropriate) during the introductions, such as what someone does for a living. Another ice breaker is to introduce people who may have a friend in common.

TALKING POINTS

MAKING THE CONVERSATION FLOW

- Talk about topics that everyone is interested in—restaurants, movies, relationships, and with caution, politics. Try to keep it light and optimistic—no one wants to get depressed at a party, and no one wants to go home angry *from* the party.

- Religion should be avoided like any one of the ten plagues.

- Unless you've just had a hurricane or a blizzard, weather is a boring topic that will put your guests to sleep. (Tip: If it doesn't, get new guests.)

- Hey, guess what? People *love* to talk about themselves, so encourage them to do so. And then encourage

yourself to really listen—there's nothing worse than daydreaming and then asking a question your guest has already answered!

• Other great topics: travel is always fun, as are medical issues (we said "issues," which doesn't include your Uncle Joe's prostate surgery!). And of course, gossip! Who doesn't like to dish? (Oh, right, the same people that like to talk about the weather!)

• Try seating people in the same industry next to one another—for sure they'll have plenty to, er, chew on. This doesn't necessarily extend to people who work *together*, however, because they usually end up talking shop to the exclusion of others.

• Working couples usually have lots to talk about with other working couples—like running their businesses, trying to organize their social lives, and getting their kids where they're supposed to be when they're supposed to be there.

• Newly separated guests? Sit them with people they know so that everyone will feel comfortable. Or better yet, sit them next to someone who loves to fix people up! If you're married, be sure that your newly single friends don't feel that they aren't as welcome now that they are no longer coupled-up.

• Okay, we're being sexist, but most women love to talk about fashion, cosmetic surgery, movies, and of course, running the country. Men on the other hand, love talking about sports, movies, and of course, running the country.

WHEN DISASTER STRIKES

Sometimes, despite your best efforts, the worst happens. Here, then, are ways to get out of the stickiest situations (and yes, that includes the sticky spills).

- As the commerical says, "never let them see you sweat." If there is a big spill, and you're part of a couple, one should handle the mess while the other entertains the guests. If you are the sole host, enlist a close friend or relative to help you out.

- Sometimes allergic reactions can't be avoided, but just to be on the safest side we always stay far away from peanut oils and sauces of any kind, and stick only to olive oil. Nut allergies can be fatal.

- Try to find out beforehand if any of your guests are vegetarian or have special dietary dictates. Big, juicy steaks and a roomful of PETA members is a bad mix.

- Have a choice of two entrées. This is important when you're grilling, especially steaks or chops. We always have a backup of baked chicken or shortribs. Why? Because Mother Nature has a way of taking things into her own hands—and out of yours and mine. And so does the outdoor grill. How many times have you ended up with meat that could pass for the charcoal that it was cooked on? Exactly. Backup!

- Speaking of backup, we keep plenty of candles handy.

As you may have guessed by now, we *love* Sundays, but even Sundays pale in comparison to holidays for us. When it's holiday time, we plan for weeks, cook for days, and eat for hours. And hours.

As restaurateurs, we obviously divide our holidays between the ones we spend at home—Christmas Day, Thanksgiving, New Year's Day, Easter Sunday, Mother's Day, and Father's Day—and those we celebrate with our patrons at Fresco. On those holidays we think of our guests as family and celebrate by cooking the same special and traditional meals we'd normally have at home.

When we say celebrate, we mean *celebrate*. On Christmas Eve, for example, we follow the menu our family has been following since the dawn of man—a feast of the Seven Fishes. And we bring in a band of strolling carolers who light up the Fresco dining room with Christmas warmth. On Valentine's Day, there's lots of red and pink and food meant for lovers—sexy food that can be shared and even finger-fed to one another. Well, you get the picture.

If you can't make it to New York City and join us at Fresco (or at home!) for the holidays, here's the next best thing—a whole host of holiday meals meant to take the stress out of cooking for a crowd. We've created menus from soup to nutty desserts, including suggestions for pairing wines with each course.

New Year's Day

PASTA E FAGIOLI
Melini Chianti Classico Riserva 1999, Tuscany

EGGPLANT AND ZUCCHINI PIE
Mastroberardino Taurasi 'Radici' 1998, Campania

BRAISED SHORT RIBS WITH ROASTED GARLIC MASHED POTATOES
Bertani Amarone della Valpolicella 1996, Venice

TOASTED PANETTONE WITH SPICED MASCARPONE AND ORANGE SUPREMES

CHOCOLATE CARROT CAKE WITH WHITE CHOCOLATE CREAM CHEESE FROSTING
Broadbent Madeira Malmsey 10-year, Portugal

Valentine's Day

**LOVE TART WITH HERB GOAT CHEESE,
ROASTED PLUM TOMATOES, AND
RED PEPPERS**
Nicolas Feuillate Rose Champagne Premier Cru NV

**RISOTTO WITH ROASTED TOMATOES,
ROASTED RED PEPPERS, TREVISANO,
AND PANCETTA**
Travaglini Gattinara 1999, Piedmont

HERB-CRUSTED BABY RACK OF LAMB

SAUTÉED SPINACH
Niebaum-Coppola 'Rubicon' Meritage 2001, Rutherford

CHOCOLATE FONDUE

**AMORE BACI CAFFÈ
(LOVE AND KISSES COFFEE)**
Masi Serego Alighieri Recioto 2001, Veneto

Easter Sunday

SAUTÉED ZUCCHINI BLOSSOMS STUFFED WITH HERBED RICOTTA CHEESE
Livio Felluga Tocai 2004, Friuli

SPRING SALAD WITH BABY SPINACH, PEAS, MINT, AND WARM GOAT CHEESE CROSTINI
Duckhorn Vineyards Sauvignon Blanc 2004, Napa

FUSILLI WITH ROASTED TOMATOES, SEASONAL MUSHROOMS, SPINACH, GARLIC, AND EXTRA-VIRGIN OLIVE OIL
Boscarelli Vino Nobile di Montepulciano 2001, Tuscany

MARINATED AND GRILLED FLANK STEAK VEGETABLE KABOBS WITH ZUCCHIHI, PEPPERS, YELLOW SQUASH, AND EGGPLANT
Sebastiani Vineyards 'Cherryblock' Cabernet Sauvignon 2001, Sonoma

---

ORANGE BLOSSOM POUND CAKE
Bonny Doons Muscat 'Vin de Glaciere' 2003, Santa Cruz

Mother's Day

**HERBAL SALAD WITH FRESH PARSLEY,
TARRAGON, CHIVE, PEEKYTOE CRAB,
AND EDIBLE FLOWERS**
Caputo Fiano Di Avellino 2004, Campania

**COLD FARRO PASTA SALAD WITH GRILLED
VEGETABLES, MOZZARELLA, PECORINO
CHEESE, AND HERB VINAIGRETTE**
Jermann Vintage Tunnina 2002, Venice

**GRILLED LOBSTER AND
SUMMER SWEET CORN**
Rudd 'Bacigalupi' Chardonnay 2003, Napa

KIWI LIME TART

LEMON ZUCCHINI BREAD
Inniskillin Riesling Ice Wine 2002, Canada

Father's Day

POTATO AND ZUCCHINI CHIPS WITH GORGONZOLA CHEESE
Michele Chiarlo Moscato D'Asti 'Nivole' 2004, Piedmont

MOZZARELLA AND TOMATO WITH BASIL SOPRESSATA, SALAMI, PROSCIUTTO, AND PARMESAN

HAND ROLLED BREAD STICKS
Feudi San Gregorio Falanghina 2004, Campania

RIGATONI WITH SUNDAY SAUCE

MEAT FROM THE SUNDAY SAUCE: MEATBALLS, PORK CHOPS, AND BRACIOLE
Castello Banfi Brunello di Montalcino Poggio All'Oro 1995, Tuscany

---

BLUEBERRY STRAWBERRY SHORTCAKE

CHOCOLATE OREO ICE CREAM PIE
Ca' dei Mandorli Brachetto D'Acqui N.V., Piedmont

Fourth of July

ITALIAN CHEESE BREAD

**HEIRLOOM TOMATO SALAD WITH BACON,
BIBB LETTUCE, AND CREAMY MAYTAG
BLUE CHEESE DRESSING**
Domaines Ott Rose Chateau de Selle 2004, Provence, France

**FETTUCCINE WITH PESTO SAUCE,
STRING BEANS, YUKON GOLD POTATOES,
AND MARIGOLD PETALS**
La Scolca Gavi di Gavi 'Black Label' 2004, Piedmont

GRILLED ASPARAGUS

**GRILLED T-BONE STEAK WITH GRILLED
RED ONIONS, RED BEANS, AND SWEET
AND HOT CHILES**
Seghesio Zinfandel Old Vines 2002, Sonoma

**GRILLED TROPICAL TART WITH PINEAPPLE,
MANGO, AND BANANA**

CHOCOLATE ZUCCHINI BREAD
Maculan Torcolato 2002, Venice

Thanksgiving Dinner

ITALIAN CHEESE BREAD

**CREAMY POLENTA WITH MASCARPONE
CHEESE**
Scarzello Dolcetto D'Alba 2003, Piedmont

**PUMPKIN GNOCCHI WITH GRATED
AMARETTI COOKIES**
Jade Mountain 'La Provencale' 2002, Napa

**HERB ROAST TURKEY WITH SAUSAGE AND
RICE STUFFING**

SWEET POTATO–STUFFED PUMPKINS
Beaux Freres Pinot Noir 2001, Oregon

PUMPKIN RICOTTA FRITTERS

SPICED PUMPKIN FUDGE
Cockburn 10-Year Tawny Port, Portugal

Christmas Eve Dinner

MARINATED SEAFOOD SALAD

CRAB CAKES WITH AVOCADO SALSA
Conundrum 2004, Oakville

GARGANELLI WITH ROCK SHRIMP, ZUCCHINI,
AND TOASTED BREAD CRUMBS
Rex Hill Pinot Gris 2004, Oregon

STEAMED MAINE MUSSELS AND MANILA CLAMS

PISTACHIO-CRUSTED SEA BASS WITH
SALSA VERDE AND ROASTED ARTICHOKES
Pio Cesare Chardonnay 'Piodilei' 2002, Piedmont

PANETTONE BREAD PUDDING

CHESTNUT CHEESECAKE WITH
CARAMEL SAUCE
Badia A Coltibuono Vin Santo 1999, Tuscany

Christmas Day

ITALIAN RICE BALLS

FRESCO'S TORTA RUSTICA
Gagliardo Fallegro 2003, Piedmont

MEATBALL LASAGNA
Angelo Gaja 'Sitorey' 1999, Piedmont

PROSCIUTTO-WRAPPED PORK CHOPS

GRILLED SIRLOIN BRACIOLES STUFFED
WITH PROVOLONE, PARMESAN, PARSLEY,
AND GARLIC
Saxum Syrah 'Bone Rock Vineyard' 2001, Paso Robles

ARBORIO RICE PUDDING

BITTERSWEET CHOCOLATE PUDDING CAKE
WITH VANILLA GELATO
Librandi Vino Passito 2003, Calabria

New Year's Eve

LENTIL SOUP
Joseph Phelps 'Le Mistral' 2001, Napa

SPIEDINI ALLA ROMANO
Taurino Salice Salentino 2001, Puglia

**CAVATELLI WITH SWEET ITALIAN SAUSAGE
AND BROCCOLI RABE**
Majara 'Milleuna' Primitivo 2001, Puglia

**STEAK PIZZAIOLA WITH SUN-DRIED TOMATO
POLENTA**
Terrabianca 'Campaccio' 2001, Tuscany

**APPLE AND PEAR CRISP WITH ALMOND
CRUMB TOPPING**
Far Niente 'Dolce' 2001, Napa

ppetizers, as the name suggests, should be like a great seduction. They are supposed to intrigue, whet the appetite, and lure the unsuspecting (or maybe the fully expecting!) into wanting more.

Appetizers, hors d'oeuvres, starters—whatever you prefer to call the opening curtain of your meal—should just *hint* at what's coming, not be an entire meal unto themselves. The last thing you want is for your guests to get so full on appetizers that they have no room left for the meal you've so lovingly prepared.

It's interesting that many people—good cooks included—think of the appetizer course as a separate entity especially when it's not served as a sit-down part of the meal, but rather during cocktails. Not us! We believe that appetizers should, and *must*, set the tone for the meal that's going to follow, not *compete* with it. Think of your courses the way you think of a color palette in your home—tone on tone.

Sure, everybody loves big old pigs-in-the-blanket, but it's not the kind of appetizer that will whet your guests' appetites for what's to follow, unless of course, you're hosting a baseball game—at the stadium.

Think complementing, not competing. Think hinting, not filling. The appetizer course should simply be the course that gets everyone warmed up for the food *and* to one another.

Naturally, the cozier, and more accessible your home is, the more at-home your guests will feel. You know what we mean—we've all been to wonderfully elegant houses that are *so* perfect that you feel there should be plastic slipcovers on the food. God forbid you drop something—will the cops show up and arrest you for wine spillage? Spills, like life, happen.

Yes, we do a huge amount of Sunday entertaining at our house in the Hamptons, and if you can't relax there, you may be genetically incapable, but still, one way we know our guests feel at home is that they invade our kitchen before dinner and make themselves at home.

You'll always find them huddled around the big island in the kitchen, peaking at what's cooking, sniffing the Sunday sauce, drinking their wine, and meeting one another.

Sure, we have a great big backyard and a lovely patio. Sure, we have our big tables set out on the lawn, and yet, our guests inevitably gravitate toward the kitchen during cocktails and appetizers. Guests and the kids usually end up perched on the high stools around the island to chat, watch the proceedings, and munch on the appetizers like Gorgonzola-smothered potato chips and pizza.

It's just the way it is, so we try to keep the cooking chaos to a minimum and the kitchen as presentable as possible. For starters, we always have a huge bouquet of flowers—mostly white Stargazers—in the middle of the work area, and even display some of the meal to whet everyone's appetite. This portion of the meal is also particularly crucial to breaking the ice. Music helps, especially when guests don't know one another. And so do fake moustaches. What? Unfortunately, we're not above putting fake moustaches on the kids and letting them serve the chips and pizzas. It gets the kids involved and not only gets everybody laughing, but also relaxed. And hey there's nothing wrong with a little cheap labor, is there?

So, let the festivities—and the food—begin! Here, then, are some of our can't-miss bits of seduction.

Grilled Pizza Margherita

❧

12 PIZZAS

4 cups lukewarm water
1 teaspoon fresh yeast
1 tablespoon molasses
2 1/2 tablespoons kosher salt
2 cups extra-virgin olive oil
3 cups all-purpose flour
3 cups high-gluten flour
1/2 cup whole-wheat flour
1 cup granted Pecorino Romano cheese
1 cup grated Bel Paese cheese
1 cup canned tomato sauce
6 tablespoons chopped fresh parsley
1/2 cup chopped fresh basil

1. In a large mixing bowl, combine the water, yeast, and molasses. Mix together gently until all the yeast dissolves. Set the mixture aside for 5 to 10 minutes until the yeast makes a raft and bubbles. Stir in the salt and 1 cup of the olive oil.

2. With the mixer on low speed, add the three kinds of flour. Mix until all the flour is absorbed and the dough pulls away from the side of the bowl. Roll the dough into one large ball and let it stand for 5 minutes.

3. Cut the dough into 12 pieces. Roll the pieces into balls and place them on an oiled baking sheet. Brush the balls lightly with olive oil and cover with plastic wrap.

4. If you are going to use the dough right away, let it sit at room temperature for 30 minutes before baking. If you don't need the dough immediately, you can store it for 1 day in the refrigerator, but you must let it sit at room temperature for 1 hour before using.

5. When the dough is ready, prepare the grill (preferably charcoal, but gas works nicely, too). Make sure the rack is set at least 4 inches from the fire.

6. On an oiled surface, push a piece of dough out using the palms (lightly oiled) of your hands. If the dough is sticking to the surface, lift it and drizzle a little more oil on the surface. You want the dough to make a 12-inch circle and be paper-thin. The shape of the pizza is not as important as the thickness of the dough.

7. Gently lift the dough, and being careful not to tear it, drape it onto the hot spot of the grill. The dough will start to rise immediately. After about 2 minutes, carefully lift the edge of the dough to see the color of the underside, which should be an even golden brown.

8. Flip the dough over and place it on the side of the grill or a cooler spot of the grill. Brush the cooked side of the dough with olive oil. Combine

the cheeses in a medium bowl. Take 2 ½ teaspoons of the combined cheese and evenly spread it out to the very edge of the dough. Next, with a tablespoon, dollop tomato sauce on the pizza (8 to 10 spoonfuls)—you don't want to spread the sauce over the whole surface of the pizza. Drizzle the pizza with 1 tablespoon of extra-virgin olive oil and sprinkle with ½ tablespoon of chopped parsley.

9. Carefully slide the pizza back to the edge of the hot section of the grill, and rotate the pizza until the bottom is evenly golden brown. This should take 3 to 4 minutes. Do not put the pizza directly over the fire, because the bottom will burn before the cheese melts.

10. Garnish with the chopped basil and serve.

Sautéed Zucchini Blossoms
Stuffed with Herbed Ricotta Cheese

❧

FOR THE CHEESE FILLING:

2 cups fresh ricotta cheese
4 ounces Parmesan cheese, freshly grated
4 ounces Pecorino Romano cheese, grated
1 pound fresh mozzarella, cut into small dice
1/4 cup chopped fresh basil
1/2 cup chopped fresh parsley
1/4 cup chopped fresh thyme
Salt and freshly ground black pepper

FOR THE ZUCCHINI BLOSSOMS:

1 cup all-purpose flour
3 eggs, beaten
3 cups bread crumbs
18 zucchini flowers, or about 1 pound
4 cups extra-virgin olive oil
Parmesan cheese

1. **TO MAKE THE CHEESE FILLING:** In a medium bowl, mix together all the ingredients, thoroughly season with salt and pepper to taste, and place in a pastry bag without a tip. If you do not have a pastry bag, you can use a small teaspoon to fill the zucchini flowers.

2. **TO MAKE THE ZUCCHINI BLOSSOMS:** In a medium bowl, combine the flour, eggs, and bread crumbs. Set aside.

3. Take each zucchini flower by the stem, gently open the flower, insert the pastry bag, and carefully squeeze the cheese filling into the flower. Be careful not to overfill the flower; leave enough of the flower at the end to fold under the whole flower. Repeat the process until all the flowers are filled.

4. Dip each blossom in the egg mixture.

5. In a 12-inch pan, heat the olive oil over medium-high heat to 325°F. Sauté 6 blossoms at a time in the oil until golden brown, about 2 minutes per side.

6. Sprinkle the tops of the blossoms with Parmesan cheese and serve hot.

Spiedini alla Romano

❦

FOR THE SPIEDINI ALLA ROMANO:

1 loaf thick-sliced Pullman or other white
  bread*
2 pounds fresh mozzarella, such as Polly-O
  or Sorrento; store brands are much
  drier than fresh
1 pack 5-inch wooden skewers
  (12 altogether)
1 cup all-purpose flour
4 eggs, lightly beaten
2 cups nonseasoned dry bread crumbs
4 cups olive oil

FOR THE ANCHOVY SAUCE:

8 anchovy fillets
1 garlic clove, crushed
3/4 cup unsalted butter
1/4 cup chopped fresh flat-leaf parsley

1. **TO MAKE THE SPIEDINI ALLA ROMANO:** Trim all the crusts from the ends and sides of the bread. Cut the bread so the pieces are the size of sticks of butter, about 2 inches by 4 inches.

2. Cut the mozzarella into the same size as the bread. Cut each piece of cheese ½ inch thick.

3. Place a slice of cheese on each slice of bread, alternating bread, cheese, bread, cheese, bread to make a double cheese sandwich.

4. Gently thread the bread and cheese sandwiches onto the skewers and flour on both sides. Flour 2 skewers at a time for easy turning. Put the eggs and bread crumbs in separate shallow bowls. Dip both sides of the sandwiches in the eggs and then in the bread crumbs.

5. Heat the olive oil to 325°F and fry sandwiches until cheese is melted and bread is golden brown.

6. **TO MAKE THE ANCHOVY SAUCE:** In a medium saucepan, combine all the ingredients and cook over medium heat until the butter melts. Do not make until ready to serve.

7. Place the sandwiches on a plate and spoon on the anchovy sauce.

*NOTE: Do not use Wonder Bread or soft, sliced, ordinary white bread. Use a firm, fresh loaf of bread with a dense quality, preferably from a neighborhood bakery.

Italian Rice Balls

❧❧

8 TO 12 RICE BALLS

4 cups cooked Arborio rice, slightly cooled
3 eggs
1/2 cup grated Romano cheese
4 ounces prosciutto, chopped
Salt
1/4 teaspoon dried oregano
1/2 teaspoon pepper
8 ounces fresh mozzarella, cubed
1 cup dried seasoned bread crumbs
2 cups frying oil

1. In a medium bowl, mix together the rice, 2 of the eggs, the Romano cheese, prosciutto, salt to taste, oregano, and pepper.

2. Place a tablespoon of the mixture in your hand and insert a cube of mozzarella into the center. Roll the rice mixture into a small ball, about 1 inch in diameter. Repeat.

3. In a small bowl, beat the remaining egg to form an egg wash. Dip each rice ball in the egg wash and then roll in the bread crumbs.

4. Heat about 1½ inches of oil to 325°F in an 8- or 10-inch skillet. Fry the rice balls about 2 minutes on each side, or until golden brown.

Panzanella Skewers with Mozzarella, Tomato, and Focaccia Bread

CR\\O

6 TO 8 SERVINGS

1 loaf focaccia bread
4 vine-ripe tomatoes or 1 pint vine-ripe
 cherry tomatoes
1 pound fresh mozzarella, cut into twelve
 1/2-inch-thick slices
1 cup whole fresh basil leaves
12 six-inch metal skewers
Extra-virgin olive oil

1. Using a sharp knife, cut the bread into twelve 2 × 2 ¾ × ¾-inch rectangles. Cut the tomatoes into slices about ¼ inch thick, and then cut them in half again. If using cherry tomatoes, leave them whole.

2. To assemble the skewers, stack a slice of bread, a slice of cheese, a basil leaf, and a tomato slice, and repeat. Place a third piece of bread on top. You will have 3 slices of bread and 2 pieces of cheese with basil and tomato in between. Secure the stack with 2 of the skewers. Repeat with the remaining ingredients until you have 4 stacks, each with 2 skewers.

3. Preheat the grill to its highest setting. Brush and clean the grill grid with a cloth, and lightly oil the grill so that the skewers will get a good sear. Grill for 1 ½ to 2 minutes per side, or until the focaccia is light brown and the cheese is melted.

4. Remove the stacks from the grill, place on a platter, and remove the metal skewers. Cut each stack in half or on the diagonal. Drizzle with olive oil and serve.

Poached Artichokes with Tomato and Onion Salad

6 SERVINGS

FOR THE ARTICHOKES:

6 garlic cloves
1 tablespoon salt
Juice of 3 lemons
6 large artichokes

FOR THE TOMATO SALAD:

2 large tomatoes, peeled, seeded, and
    cut into 1/4-inch dice
1 medium red onion, diced
3 tablespoons chopped fresh basil
1/4 cup extra-virgin olive oil, plus more
    for drizzling
1/4 cup balsamic vinegar
Kosher salt and freshly ground black
    pepper

1. **TO MAKE THE ARTICHOKES:** In a large pot, combine 2 quarts of water, the garlic, salt, and lemon juice.

2. Prepare the artichokes by snipping off the thorny ends of the leaves. Push the leaves apart to expose the choke. Use a teaspoon to scoop out and discard the choke. Place the artichokes in the lemon water and bring to a boil. Simmer over medium heat for about 1 hour, or until the artichokes are tender.

3. Remove from the heat and set aside for 30 minutes to allow the artichokes to cool.

4. **TO MAKE THE TOMATO SALAD:** In a large bowl, combine the tomatoes, onion, basil, olive oil, vinegar, and salt and pepper to taste.

5. Spoon the tomato salad into the centers of the artichokes. Drizzle olive oil over the top and serve.

Creamy Polenta with Chicken Liver Ragu, Pancetta, Caramelized Onions, and Wild Mushrooms

4 TO 6 SERVINGS

FOR THE POLENTA:

3 cups milk
1 cup water
1 cup instant polenta
1/2 cup mascarpone

FOR THE RAGU:

4 or 5 large fresh chanterelle or porcini
 mushrooms, sliced
3 tablespoons olive oil
3 tablespoons butter
1 white onion, cut into small dice
1 pound fresh chicken livers
Salt and freshly ground black pepper
1/4 cup Cognac
1/2 cup veal stock

1. **TO MAKE THE POLENTA:** In a large pot over medium heat, bring the milk and water to a boil, then slowly add the polenta. Lower the heat and stir constantly for 6 to 7 minutes, or until the liquid has been absorbed.

2. Remove the pot from the heat and stir in the mascarpone. Set the polenta aside.

3. **TO MAKE THE RAGU:** In a medium sauté pan over medium heat, sauté the mushrooms in 1 tablespoon of the olive oil until tender, about 2 minutes. Set the mushrooms aside on a plate. Add 1 tablespoon of the butter and 1 tablespoon olive oil to the pan and sauté the onion until soft and tender, about 3 minutes. Add the onions to the plate with the mushrooms.

4. Trim the fat from the chicken livers, separate the two lobes, and cut any attaching veins. Season the livers with salt and pepper to taste. Sauté the prepared livers in the remaining 2 tablespoons of butter and 1 tablespoon olive oil over medium-high heat for 2 to 3 minutes until they are browned and just cooked.

5. Set the livers aside on a separate plate and keep warm. Add the mushrooms and onions to the sauté pan, add the Cognac and sauté for 1 or 2 minutes to cook off the alcohol, then add the veal stock. Reduce the sauce slightly, season with salt and pepper to taste, and add the chicken livers. Serve the ragu over the cooked polenta.

Lentil Soup

❧

8 SERVINGS

¼ cup extra-virgin olive oil
4 Italian sausage links, cut into ½-inch rounds
1 large carrot, peeled and cut into small dice
¼ cup minced onion
2 garlic cloves, smashed and minced
1 celery stalk, peeled and cut into small dice
1 ½ cups crushed canned tomatoes
1 pound dried lentils
8 cups water
Salt and freshly ground black pepper

1. Heat the olive oil in a large soup pot or Dutch oven and sauté the sausage over medium heat, until brown, about 5 minutes.

2. Add the carrot, onion, garlic, and celery and sauté until the onions are translucent, about 5 minutes. Add the crushed tomatoes, lentils, and the water and season with salt and pepper to taste. Cover and simmer for 1 hour, or until the lentils are tender.

Potato and Zucchini Chips with Gorgonzola Cheese

❧

6 SERVINGS

1 pound large baking potatoes
½ pound large zucchini
2 tablespoons all-purpose flour
2 quarts peanut oil for frying
Kosher salt
1 cup crumbled Gorgonzola cheese

1. Peel the potatoes and cut them into very thin slices. Immediately put the slices in a bowl of cold water.

2. Cut the zucchini into thin slices, place them in a large bowl, and toss with the flour. Drain the potatoes and dry on paper towels.

3. In a heavy sauté pan, heat the oil to 325°F. Deep-fry the potato and zucchini chips until golden brown, 2 to 3 minutes. Drain, season with salt to taste, and let cool.

4. Preheat the oven to 350°F. Place the potato and zucchini chips on a large baking pan and sprinkle with the Gorgonzola cheese. Bake until the cheese melts, about 5 minutes.

Fresco's Torta Rustica

❧

FOR THE CHEESE FILLING:

3 large eggs
1/2 cup shredded cheddar cheese
1 cup shredded mozzarella cheese
1/2 cup shredded Swiss cheese
2 pounds ricotta cheese
6 tablespoons grated Romano cheese
1/2 teaspoon black pepper
1/2 pound prosciutto, finely diced
Salt

FOR THE DOUGH:

3 cups flour
1 pinch salt
1 cup cold unsalted butter, cut into
    small pieces
1/4 cup ice water
1 egg yolk, slightly beaten

1. **TO MAKE THE CHEESE FILLING:** Add all the ingredients to a large bowl and mix until smooth.

2. **TO MAKE THE DOUGH:** In a large mixing bowl, combine the flour and salt. Cut in the butter until the mixture resembles coarse cornmeal. Add the ice water and mix just until the dough comes together. Wrap in plastic and refrigerate for 30 minutes.

3. Preheat the oven to 350°F. Cut the dough in half and roll out the two separate pieces. Use one to line the bottom and sides of a 10-inch springform pan. Put the cheese filling into the pan. Roll out the remaining dough into a 10-inch circle, place on top of the filling, and brush with the egg yolk. Puncture the top crust in several places with a sharp knife and bake for 1 hour, or until the crust is golden brown.

Italian Cheese Bread

❧

6 SERVINGS

1 loaf Italian bread, sliced 1/2 inch thick
1 cup extra-virgin olive oil
8 ounces Parmigiano Reggiano, grated

1. Preheat the oven to 350°F. Using a pastry brush, coat each slice of bread on both sides with olive oil.

2. Sprinkle a teaspoon of the Parmigiano Reggiano onto each slice of bread.

3. Place the bread slices on a baking sheet and bake for 3 to 5 minutes until the cheese bubbles and melts. Serve warm.

Wild Mushroom and Chickpea Soup with Spareribs

6 SERVINGS

2 ounces dried porcini or other wild
  mushrooms
1/2 cup dry white wine
4 tablespoons olive oil
8 pork spareribs (about 1 1/2 pounds), cut
  into individual pieces
1 large onion, cut into 1/2-inch dice
3 large garlic cloves, minced
1/4 cup finely minced fresh flat-leaf parsley
2 large potatoes, peeled and cut into
  1/2-inch dice
Two 15 1/2-ounces cans chickpeas, rinsed
  and drained
6 ounces fresh cremini or other mushrooms,
  cleaned and thinly sliced
7 cups water
Salt and freshly ground black pepper
1/2 cup finely minced fresh basil

1. In a small bowl, soak the porcini mushrooms in the wine for 30 minutes to soften them. Remove the mushrooms with a slotted spoon and reserve the wine. Finely chop the mushrooms and set them aside.

2. In a large soup pot or Dutch oven over medium heat, heat the olive oil and add the spareribs. Sauté until they are lightly browned on all sides, about 10 minutes, turning the ribs occasionally. Add the onion and sauté until softened, about 3 minutes. Add the garlic, stir well, and cook 1 minute.

3. Add the dried mushrooms, wine, parsley, potatoes, chickpeas, fresh mushrooms, water, and salt and pepper to taste. Bring to a boil over medium heat. Reduce the heat to a very slow but steady simmer and cook, covered, until the spareribs are very tender, about 2 hours. Stir frequently but gently.

4. Serve hot, with a sparerib placed to the side of each bowl so the bone is evident. Sprinkle basil over each serving.

Sweet Potato White Bean Soup

❧

6 TO 8 SERVINGS

¼ cup olive oil

¼ pound pancetta, finely diced (about ½ cup)

3 carrots, finely diced (about 1 cup)

1 onion, finely diced (about 1 cup)

1 small fennel bulb, trimmed and finely diced (about 1 cup)

2 tablespoons chopped garlic

1 pound dried navy beans, rinsed and picked over

2 tablespoons chopped fresh rosemary

1 teaspoon kosher salt, plus more for seasoning

1 teaspoon crushed red pepper flakes

3 quarts chicken stock

3 sweet potatoes, peeled and cut into 1-inch cubes (about 4 cups)

½ cup freshly grated Parmesan cheese

1. In a large stockpot or Dutch oven, heat the olive oil over medium-low heat. Add the pancetta and cook, uncovered, for 20 to 30 minutes, or until the fat is rendered.

2. Add the carrots, onion, fennel, garlic, beans, rosemary, salt, red pepper flakes, stock, and 4 to 6 cups of water. Bring to a boil over medium-high heat, then reduce the heat to medium and simmer for about 1 hour, uncovered, or until the beans are cooked al dente.

3. Add the sweet potatoes and Parmesan cheese and simmer for about 20 minutes, or until the potatoes are tender and the beans are soft.

4. Ladle 3 cups of the soup, both the solids and broth, into a food processor fitted with the metal blade and puree. Return to the pot and heat through. Season with additional salt if necessary and serve.

Acqua Cotta

∾

6 SERVINGS

1/2 pound escarole
1/4 cup olive oil
2 cups minced onion
2 cups minced carrots
1 cup minced celery
2 tablespoons chopped garlic
1 to 2 teaspoons crushed red pepper
   flakes
1 tablespoon chopped fresh sage
1 teaspoon chopped fresh rosemary
3 tablespoons chopped fresh flat-leaf
   parsley
2 pounds plum tomatoes, peeled, seeded,
   and chopped
5 cups water
1/2 cup freshly grated Parmesan cheese,
   plus rind
Kosher salt
6 slices Tuscan bread or other peasant-
   style bread
1 or 2 garlic cloves, peeled
6 large eggs
2 tablespoons extra-virgin olive oil

1. In a large pot of boiling water, blanch the escarole for about 1 minute, or until barely wilted. Using a slotted spoon, transfer the escarole to a bowl of cold water for a few seconds to set the color. Shake off the excess water and transfer it to a plate. Set aside.

2. In a large stockpot, heat the 1/4 cup olive oil over medium heat. Add the onion, carrots, celery, chopped garlic, red pepper flakes, sage, rosemary, and parsley and cook, stirring frequently, for 20 to 25 minutes, or until the vegetables soften.

3. Add the tomatoes and cook 15 to 20 minutes more, or until the tomatoes are so soft they fall apart. Add the water, escarole, and cheese rind. Bring the soup to a simmer over medium heat, and cook for 20 minutes, or until the cheese rind breaks up and the soup thickens slightly. Pull out the rind if it is solid and discard. Season to taste with salt.

4. Toast the bread until lightly browned and rub the slices with the garlic cloves. Place a slice of toast in each of 6 serving bowls.

5. Reduce the heat to medium-low, but keep the soup simmering. Carefully crack 1 egg into a cup, keeping the yolk whole. Slide the egg into the simmering soup using a small strainer or slotted spoon as support. Repeat with the remaining eggs, cooking each egg for 2 to 3 minutes, or until poached.

6. Lift each poached egg from the pot using the strainer or slotted spoon and position it on a piece of toast. Ladle some of the hot broth and vegetables over each. Drizzle each bowl with 1 teaspoon of the extra-virgin olive oil and garnish with the grated Parmesan.

*O*ur ancestors—the ones who first came to the United States—would be very amused indeed to hear that the salads that are considered so upscale and fancy today were the very salads they used to make as new immigrants.

Yes, believe it or not, mozzarella and tomato salad sprinkled with Italian olive oil (caprese salad) was at one time considered "peasant food." That's probably because new Italian immigrants could always be found eating it. They loved it not only because it was inexpensive, but because it was a delicious way to bring a bit of the old country to the new one. Nowadays caprese is practically considered designer food. But to us, it's just one of the delicious salads we all grew up with.

Because we love the salad portion of our Sunday dinners so much, we spend lots of time figuring out new and fun ways to mix and match ingredients, taking full advantage of the seasons. In summer we *love* a salad made up of watermelon and red onions. It not only looks like a perfect summer day—all ablaze and cool at the same time—but it's incredibly refreshing.

Watermelon at an Italian dinner? You bet! In fact, in Italy on hot summer nights, the busiest places in town are generally the crazy watermelon stands set up in most cities, big and small.

Ahh, but salad isn't just for cooling off. Sometimes it can be cozy comfort food on a brisk chilly afternoon as well. For example, in autumn, we love to add crunchy walnuts, apples, and Gorgonzola cheese to our favorite green salads. Another Scotto Sunday favorite is roasted pumpkin and beetroot salad with goat cheese and roasted pumpkin seeds.

Our only requirements? Have fun, be creative, and for goodness sake, think outside the produce box!

Autumn Salad of Apples, Gorgonzola, and Toasted Walnuts
with Walnut Oil Vinaigrette

❧

6 SERVINGS

FOR THE WALNUT OIL VINAIGRETTE:

3 tablespoons red wine or sherry vinegar
2 teaspoons Dijon mustard
3/4 cup walnut oil
Salt and freshly ground black pepper

FOR THE SALAD:

1/2 cup walnut halves
6 to 8 ounces blue cheese (Gorgonzola Dolce, Stilton, or Roquefort), crumbled or cut into 1/2-inch square chunks
3 heads Belgian endive or frisée, trimmed and separated into leaves
1 head radicchio or Trevisano, cut into 1-inch pieces or separated into leaves
2 bunches watercress or arugula, tough stems removed and rinsed thoroughly
2 to 3 apples (preferably Gala or Spy) skin on, halved, cored, and cut lengthwise into 1/8-inch slices

1. **TO MAKE THE WALNUT OIL VINAIGRETTE:** In a small bowl, whisk the vinegar and mustard. Slowly whisk in the oil until the dressing becomes creamy. Season with salt and pepper to taste. Set aside until ready to use.

2. **TO MAKE THE SALAD:** Preheat the oven to 350°F. Place the walnuts on a cookie sheet and toast them until they are lightly browned, crisp, and smell rich, 10 to 14 minutes.

3. In a large bowl, toss the walnuts, cheese, endive, radicchio, and watercress.

4. Dress the salad with the vinaigrette and toss lightly to coat.

5. Season with salt and pepper to taste and garnish with the sliced apples.

NOTE: *As a variation, pears, such as D'Anjou or Bartlett, may be substituted for the apples.*

Herbal Salad with Fresh Parsley, Tarragon, Chive, Peekytoe Crab, and Edible Flowers

❧

4 SERVINGS

FOR THE LEMON DRESSING (MAKES 1 3/4 CUP):

Scant 1/2 cup lemon juice
2 teaspoons grain mustard
1 tablespoon minced fresh thyme
1/2 cup vegetable oil
1/2 cup extra-virgin olive oil
Salt and freshly ground black pepper

FOR THE SALAD:

1/4 cup chopped fresh flat-leaf parsley
1/4 cup chopped fresh tarragon
1/4 cup chopped fresh chives
1 pound fresh Peekytoe crabmeat, cleaned
1 head romaine lettuce, chopped into 1-inch pieces
4 ounces edible flowers, such as pansies

1. **TO MAKE THE LEMON DRESSING:** Place the lemon juice, mustard, and thyme in a medium bowl, and whisk in the oils until smooth. Season with salt and pepper to taste.

2. **TO MAKE THE SALAD:** Place the parsley, tarragon, and chives in a small bowl. Add the crabmeat and half the lemon dressing and toss well.

3. Layer the crabmeat about 1 inch thick on a round dinner plate. Cover the crab with the lettuce. Layer the remaining crabmeat on top of the lettuce.

4. Pour on the rest of the lemon dressing and season with salt and pepper to taste. Garnish with the edible flowers.

Grilled Cotoletta of Chicken Breast, Spring Vegetables, and Baby Lettuce Salad with Lemon Herb Vinaigrette

FOR THE CHICKEN AND VEGETABLES:

1 bunch fresh green asparagus, peeled and trimmed*
1/2 pound French string beans, strings removed
1/2 pound peeled baby carrots
4 ears corn, shucked
1 small red onion, peeled and sliced into 1/4-inch rings
Olive oil
1/2 pint red and yellow cherry tomatoes, split in half
4 fresh radishes, sliced very thin
1/2 pint sugar snap peas, string removed
Six 6- to 7-ounce boneless chicken breasts, butterflied

FOR THE SALAD:

1 pound fresh spring baby lettuce mix or your own mix of young arugula, frisée, romaine hearts, radicchio, and Bibb lettuces
Juice of 6 to 7 freshly squeezed lemons
1 teaspoon Dijon mustard
1 teaspoon honey
1/2 cup extra-virgin olive oil
1 tablespoon chopped fresh dill
1 tablespoon chopped fresh basil
1 tablespoon chopped fresh chervil
Salt and freshly ground black pepper

1. **TO MAKE THE CHICKEN AND VEGETABLES:** Blanch the asparagus, French beans, and carrots in boiling salted water for 2 minutes, or just until crisp.

2. To keep the vegetables from overcooking and losing their color, immediately cool them in an ice bath. Drain and set aside to dry.

3. Preheat the grill. Brush the corn and red onion with olive oil and grill just until tender. Let the corn cool, then, standing each cob on its end, use a knife to slice straight down the cob, removing the corn kernels.

4. Cut the asparagus into 2-inch lengths and split the carrots in half.

5. In a large stainless steel bowl, mix together the asparagus, French beans, carrots, corn, red onions, tomatoes, radishes, and snap peas. Refrigerate.

6. Place each breast between 2 sheets of plastic wrap and pound it to about 1/4 inch thick. Place the chicken on the grill and cook about 3 minutes per side, or until cooked through. Place the chicken on a serving platter.

7. **TO MAKE THE SALAD:** Add the baby lettuces to the bowl with the vegetables.

8. In a small bowl whisk, together the lemon juice, mustard, honey, and olive oil. Add the fresh herbs** and season with salt and pepper to taste.

9. Toss the salad with the lemon vinaigrette. Place the mixed salad on top of the grilled chicken and serve.

*NOTE: *If the asparagus are pencil-thin, there's no need to peel them, just trim 2 inches off the base.*
**NOTE: *Do not add the herbs to the vinaigrette until the salad is ready to be served.*

Spring Salad with Baby Spinach, Peas, Mint, and Warm Goat Cheese Crostini

❧

6 SERVINGS

FOR THE LEMON DRESSING (MAKES 3/4 CUP):

Scant 1/2 cup freshly squeezed lemon juice
2 teaspoons grain mustard
1 tablespoon minced fresh thyme leaves
1/2 cup vegetable oil
1/2 cup extra-virgin olive oil, plus extra
    for garnish
Salt and freshly ground black pepper

FOR THE SALAD:

1 cup freshly podded peas
1 cup sugar snap peas
5 ounces fresh baby spinach leaves
1/4 cup chopped fresh basil leaves
1/4 cup chopped fresh mint leaves
1/2 cup fresh flat-leaf parsley leaves
2 tablespoons sliced green onion

FOR THE CROSTINI:

1 loaf sliced Italian bread or ficelle (thin
    loaf French bread)
6 ounces goat cheese (or fresh goat curd)
Extra-virgin olive oil
Freshly ground black pepper

1. **TO MAKE THE LEMON DRESSING:** In a medium bowl, place the lemon juice, mustard, and thyme. Whisk in the oils, then season with salt and pepper to taste.

2. **TO MAKE THE SALAD:** Blanch the podded peas and snap peas briefly in boiling salted water; refresh in ice water, and drain. In a large bowl, combine the spinach, peas, basil, mint, parsley, and onion. Toss with enough lemon dressing to coat lightly.

3. **TO MAKE THE CROSTINI:** Preheat the grill to high heat. Toast the bread slices on the hot grill until marked on each side, about 1 minute per side, then spread them with the goat cheese. Lower the grill's heat and warm the bread through.

4. To serve, place a portion of the salad in the center of each plate. Place 2 goat cheese crostini beside each salad, drizzle a little olive oil over the goat cheese, and top with pepper.

Fried Oyster Salad

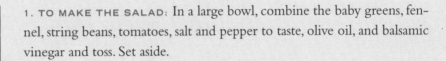

6 SERVINGS

FOR THE SALAD:

1 pound mixed baby greens
1 tablespoon julienned fennel
3/4 pound baby string beans, blanched
8 cherry tomatoes, cut in half
Salt and freshly ground black pepper
3/4 cup extra-virgin olive oil
1/4 cup balsamic vinegar

FOR THE FRIED OYSTERS:

1 cup all-purpose flour
3 egg whites
Salt and freshly ground black pepper
1/2 cup beer
18 fresh oysters, shells reserved
2 cups vegetable or other frying oil

1. **TO MAKE THE SALAD:** In a large bowl, combine the baby greens, fennel, string beans, tomatoes, salt and pepper to taste, olive oil, and balsamic vinegar and toss. Set aside.

2. **TO MAKE THE FRIED OYSTERS:** In a bowl, combine the flour, egg whites, and salt and pepper to taste. Mix well. Pour the beer in slowly and mix well. Set the batter aside.

3. Open the oysters and save the shells. Dip the oysters in the batter. Heat the frying oil to 375°F, and fry the oysters until they are brown and crisp on the outside, about 3 minutes.

4. To serve, divide the salad among 6 plates and top each with 2 fried oysters and a third fried oyster on the half shell.

Watermelon and Red Onion Salad with Watercress and Muscat Vinaigrette

6 SERVINGS

3 bunches watercress
2 red onions, sliced paper thin
1/4 cup Muscat or white balsamic vinegar
Salt and cracked black pepper
1/2 cup extra-virgin olive oil
5 cups seedless or seeded red and yellow
　　watermelon

1. Trim the stems of the watercress. Rinse the watercress and dry it thoroughly. Keep the watercress chilled until you are ready to assemble the salad.

2. Place the sliced onions in ice water and soak them for at least 30 minutes to 1 hour; overnight is even better.

3. In a small bowl, combine the vinegar and salt and pepper to taste. Whisk in the olive oil.

4. Place the watermelon, watercress, and red onion in a large bowl and dress with the vinaigrette. Check the seasoning and add salt and pepper to taste. Place the salad on plates or a large platter.

NOTE: *The colder all the ingredients are, the better. Watermelon is always best ice cold.*

Marinated Seafood Salad

2 cups white wine

1 1/2 tablespoons black peppercorns

3 garlic cloves

2 bay leaves

Juice of 1 lemon

2 pounds octopus (will shrink by half when cooked)

1 pound medium shrimp, peeled and deveined

1 pound calamari, cleaned and cut into rings

1 pound lump crabmeat

1/2 cup julienned carrots

1/2 cup julienned onions

1/2 cup julienned celery

1/2 cup extra-virgin olive oil, plus additional for garnish

1/2 cup chopped garlic

1/2 cup chopped fresh flat-leaf parsley

1 orange, segmented, pith and peel removed

2 cups pulp-free orange juice

Salt and freshly ground black pepper

1. In a large pot, place the wine, peppercorns, garlic cloves, bay leaves, lemon juice, and 3 quarts of water. Bring the liquid to a boil over high heat, then lower the heat so that the liquid is at a simmer. Add the octopus and simmer for 45 minutes, or until tender. Remove from the heat and let the octopus cool in the liquid. Remove the octopus from the liquid, cover, and refrigerate. This step can be done 2 days in advance.

2. Bring the liquid to a simmer again, add the shrimp and calamari and cook for 3 minutes, or until the shrimp turn pink. Let them cool in the liquid, remove them, cover, and refrigerate.

3. Using the same water, parboil the carrots, onions, and celery for 1 minute. Drain and cool the vegetables.

4. Remove the soft purple skin and suckers from the octopus. In a small bowl, combine the olive oil, chopped garlic, and parsley. Marinate the octopus in the parsley mixture in refrigerator for 1 hour.

5. Preheat the grill to high. Add the octopus and grill for 10 minutes, or until tender. Cut the octopus into 1/4-inch pieces.

6. In a large bowl, combine the seafood, vegetables, orange segments, and orange juice and marinate for at least 12 hours before serving. Add salt, pepper, and olive oil to taste.

Heirloom Tomato Salad with Bacon, Bibb Lettuce, and Creamy Maytag Blue Cheese Dressing

❧

6 SERVINGS

FOR THE CHEESE DRESSING:

7 ounces Maytag blue cheese, crumbled
2 cups mayonnaise
1/2 cup sour cream
3/4 cup buttermilk
1 tablespoon lemon juice
2 teaspoons Worcestershire sauce
3 dashes Tabasco sauce
2 teaspoons salt
1 teaspoon freshly ground black pepper
3 tablespoons minced fresh chives

FOR THE SALAD:

3 heads Bibb lettuce, washed and chilled
4 pounds heirloom tomatoes of varying
    size, flavor, and color
Salt and freshly ground black pepper
1/4 cup extra-virgin olive oil
1/2 pound smoked bacon, cooked until
    crisp

1. **TO MAKE THE CHEESE DRESSING:** In a large mixing bowl, mix together the cheese, mayonnaise, sour cream, and buttermilk.

2. Add the lemon juice, Worcestershire, Tabasco, salt, and pepper. If the dressing is too thick, thin with more buttermilk. Finish the dressing by adding the chives.

3. **TO MAKE THE SALAD:** Separate the leaves of lettuce, keeping them whole.

4. Cut the tomatoes in 1/4-inch slices. Season with salt and pepper and a sprinkle of olive oil.

5. Line 6 plates with the lettuce. Give each person a stack of tomatoes 3 to 4 inches high, with the largest slices on the bottom. Alternate colors and place the smaller slices on top. Top each stack with creamy dressing and decorate with bacon, either by leaving the pieces whole or crumbling.

Cold Farro Pasta Salad with Grilled Vegetables, Mozzarella, Pecorino Cheese, and Herb Vinaigrette

6 SERVINGS

FOR THE HERB VINAIGRETTE:

1 cup chopped fresh basil
1/2 cup minced fresh chives
2 tablespoons minced garlic
2 tablespoons minced shallots
1 cup extra-virgin olive oil
1/4 cup balsamic vinegar
Salt and freshly ground black pepper

FOR THE PASTA SALAD:

1/2 pound asparagus tips
2 medium zucchini, cut into 1/2-inch slices
1 large red onion, peeled and cut into
　1/2-inch slices
2 red peppers, seeded and cut in half
　lengthwise
1/4 cup extra-virgin olive oil
1 pound uncooked farro pasta
1/2 pound diced mozzarella
1/4 cup grated Pecorino cheese
Salt and freshly ground black pepper

1. **TO MAKE THE HERB VINAIGRETTE:** In a medium bowl, combine the basil, chives, garlic, and shallots and whisk in the oil and vinegar. Season to taste with salt and pepper.

2. **TO MAKE THE PASTA SALAD:** Brush the asparagus, zucchini, and onion lightly with the olive oil. Place the vegetables on a hot grill and cook until light brown and tender, about 3 minutes. Remove from the grill, dice, and place in a large bowl.

3. Cook the farro pasta in a large pot of bowling water until al dente about 8 to 10 minutes. Drain and cool.

4. Add the farro pasta to the cooked vegetables.

5. Place the pasta and vegetables on a platter and drizzle with the herb vinaigrette. Top with the diced mozzarella and grated Pecorino cheese. Serve at room temperature or cold.

Roasted Pumpkin and Beetroot Salad with Goat Cheese and Toasted Pumpkin Seeds

6 SERVINGS

3 large red or gold beets
Salt and freshly ground black pepper
3 cups cheese pumpkin, peeled, seeded, and cut into 2-inch chunks
Olive oil
1/2 cup pumpkin seeds
2 shallots, finely minced
1/4 cup sherry vinegar
1/4 cup extra-virgin olive oil
3 cups mixed greens
One 6-ounce log fresh goat cheese, cut into 6 equal rounds

1. Preheat the oven to 400°F.

2. In a small saucepan, cover the beets with cold water. Season with salt and pepper to taste, and bring the water to a boil over high heat. Reduce the heat and simmer for 25 minutes, or until the beets are tender when pierced with a tip of a small, sharp knife. Drain the beets and set aside to cool. Peel and slice the beets into ⅛-inch rounds.

3. While the beets are simmering, season the pumpkin with salt, pepper, and olive oil, and wrap in foil. Roast for 20 to 30 minutes, or until tender. Unwrap the pumpkin and cool. Cut the pumpkin into ½-inch pieces and set aside.

4. While the pumpkin cooks, rinse the pumpkin seeds and spread in a single layer on a baking sheet. Sprinkle with 1 teaspoon of salt. Bake for 5 minutes or until light brown. Set the toasted seeds aside.

5. In a small bowl, whisk together the shallots, vinegar, extra-virgin olive oil, and salt and pepper to taste. Place the salad greens in a large bowl and toss with a few tablespoons of the dressing, just enough to coat the leaves.

6. Arrange the beet slices in a circular pattern on a large round platter. Place the roasted pumpkin in a circle on top of beets. Place the salad greens in the center of the beet circle. Place the goat cheese disks around the outside of the salad between the beets and greens and sprinkle the toasted pumpkin seeds over the top of the salad. Spoon the remaining vinaigrette over the beets and pumpkin.

ow we come to the heart, the soul, the *stomach* of our Sunday dinner—the pasta and/or risotto course. Not to be overly dramatic, but can there even *be* Sunday without pasta? The answer is self-evident: absolutely not! Pasta is like life—it shouldn't fill you up so much as give you a reason to go on. As you might have guessed, we take our Sunday sauce and pasta course (or as the old folks used to call it "macaroni and gravy") very seriously. Pasta and its creamy cousin risotto are what put the "comfort" in comfort food. It's no mistake that "pasta" ends in "ah," you know. It's the one food *guaranteed* to put a smile on everyone's face—no matter what.

Take the near disaster at our house one Sunday, when actor Ben Gazzara hit the sauce—or more accurately, when pasta sauce hit Ben Gazzara. Rosanna was about twelve years old and doing double duty as waitress (as we said, the parents went for the cheap labor!). She was trying to serve, when she instead spilled hot sauce down the back of Mr. Gazzara's shirt. She was mortified! And Ben? Definitely more forgiving than he should have been. We always laugh when we think of that story, because we knew she had gotten a pass. Was it good manners on his part, or was it the pasta that made him so forgiving? Probably both. But seriously, how could anyone stay angry when faced (or hit in the back) with our pasta and Sunday sauce?

If you're looking for a smile, or a little down-home comfort, Italian style, think pasta. May we recommend penne gratin? Or cavatelli with Italian sausage and broccoli rabe? Sunday sauce with meat? Only in need of comfort lite? Try the pasta with zucchini Calabrian style. Need a serious comfort fix? The Rx is risotto. Right away. Yes, it takes a bit more patience than pasta, but the payoff is worth it. While most people consider risotto a winter dish, we serve it all year long—especially risotto with snap peas and fava beans. Ahhh.

Remember, contrary to popular misconception, pasta and risotto are healthful, hearty, happy foods, which is why we consider them a food group unto themselves! So, stop feeling guilty about eating well—and *mangiare la pasta!*

Pasta and Risotto

[CONTINUED]

Fresco Timpano

֍

6 SERVINGS

1 pound uncooked penne pasta
Salt
1 1/2 pounds sweet Italian sausage,
  removed from casing
2 tablespoons chopped garlic
4 tablespoons olive oil
2 eggplants, skinned and diced
1 cup sweet peas
2 cups diced tomatoes
1 bunch fresh basil, stems removed and
  leaves chopped
2 1/2 cups tomato sauce (see recipe on
  page 100)
1 1/4 pounds fresh ricotta cheese
1 cup grated Parmesan cheese
1/2 pound fresh mozzarella, diced
Freshly ground black pepper
2 tablespoons all-purpose flour
2 puff pastry sheets
4 tablespoons butter
2 egg yolks, lightly beaten

1. Cook the pasta in salted boiling water until al dente, about 8 minutes. Drain and set aside.

2. In a sauté pan over high heat, cook the sausage, garlic, and 2 tablespoons of the oil until the meat is crispy. Drain the oil.

3. In another pan over medium heat, heat the remaining 2 tablespoons oil and sauté the eggplants until crispy, or about 5 minutes.

4. In a large bowl, mix together the peas, tomatoes, basil, sausage, and eggplant.

5. Add 2 cups of the tomato sauce and fold in the ricotta, Parmesan, mozzarella, and penne. Add salt and pepper to taste.

6. Preheat the oven to 325°F. Sprinkle the flour on the puff pastry sheets and roll out into 9-inch diameter circles.

7. Rub the butter on the bottom and sides of a 12-inch springform pan. Line the pan with one pastry sheet and fill it with the penne mixture.

8. Cover the pan with the other pastry sheet, making sure that none of the stuffing is left uncovered. Brush the top of the pastry with the egg yolks and bake for about 30 minutes, or until golden brown. Warm the remaining 1/2 cup tomato sauce. Cut the timpano into wedges and top with the warmed sauce. Serve hot.

Whole Wheat Penne with Braised Beets,
Gorgonzola Cheese, and Walnuts

4 to 5 whole beets, stems and greens removed and reserved

1/2 teaspoon salt, plus additional for seasoning

5 tablespoons extra-virgin olive oil

1 large onion, diced small (about 1 cup)

4 garlic cloves, thinly sliced

Freshly ground black pepper

3 cups water or chicken stock

1 pound uncooked whole wheat rigatoni or penne

1 cup crumbled Gorgonzola or goat cheese

3/4 cup whole walnuts

1. Place the beets in a medium pot and cover with water. Season with the 1/2 teaspoon salt and simmer over medium heat until the beets are cooked through, about 1 hour or slightly more. Check if the beets are ready by piercing them with a paring knife; there should be little to no resistance. Remove the beets from the pot and cool on a plate for 15 to 20 minutes. Remove the beet skin by rubbing the beets with paper towels, then rinse them lightly under cool water to remove any skin particles. Cut the beets into large dice and reserve in a covered bowl until the pasta is prepared.

2. Stem the beet greens and cut the leaves crosswise into ribbons. Cut the stems in half lengthwise on the bias. Rinse the greens and stems under running water until all the grit and sand is removed.

3. In a medium sauté pan over medium heat, heat the olive oil and sauté the onion until golden brown, about 5 minutes. Add the garlic and sauté for another 5 minutes. Season with salt and pepper to taste. Add the greens, beet stems, and stock and simmer gently until tender, 20 to 30 minutes. Remove from the heat and add the diced beets.

4. Meanwhile, cook the pasta in salted boiling water until it is al dente, about 8 to 10 minutes. Strain, but do not rinse. Combine the pasta and beet mixture together in the pasta pan. Just before serving, fold in the cheese and walnuts, and add salt and pepper to taste.

Sunday Sauce with Meatballs, Sausages, and Pork Chops

❧

TOTAL COOKING TIME: 2 HOURS AND 15 MINUTES
8 TO 10 SERVINGS

1/2 cup extra-virgin olive oil
1 pound mild sausage
1/2 pound hot Italian sausage
6 thinly sliced pork chops (about 3 pounds)
2 cups dry red wine
2 tablespoons chopped garlic
2 onions, diced
1 cup diced pancetta
1 tablespoon crushed red pepper
1 gallon canned Italian plum tomatoes, undrained
2 cups chopped fresh basil
2 pounds cooked meatballs (see recipe on page 104)
2 pounds uncooked rigatoni pasta

1. In a large pot over medium heat, heat the oil and sauté the sausages and pork chops until brown, about 10 minutes. Don't worry if the meat is not cooked through because it will finish in the sauce. Remove the meat from the pan and set aside. Keep pan over medium heat. Deglaze the pan by adding 1 cup of the wine and scraping up the bits.

2. In the same pot, add the garlic, onions, pancetta, and crushed pepper and cook until the onions and garlic are lightly browned, about 2 minutes. Add the remaining 1 cup of red wine and cook until the mixture is reduced by half. Add the tomatoes and simmer for 1 hour over low heat.

3. Add the basil, sausages, pork chops, and meatballs to the tomato sauce, and simmer for 1 more hour over low heat.

4. In a large pot of boiling, salted water, cook the pasta for 10 to 12 minutes or until al dente. Drain the pasta, toss it with the Sunday Sauce, and serve immediately.

Pasta with Zucchini Calabrian Style with Caramelized Onions, Lemon Zest, and Bread Crumbs

6 SERVINGS

3/4 cup extra-virgin olive oil

Salt and freshly ground black pepper

2 ounces unseasoned bread crumbs
(8 tablespoons)

1 1/2 cups diced sweet onion

Grated zest of 1 lemon

2 to 3 pounds small to medium zucchini,
cut into medium dice

4 garlic cloves, sliced paper thin

1 pound uncooked fusilli pasta

1. Heat ¼ cup of the oilve oil in a sauté pan over low heat. Season with salt and pepper to taste, add the bread crumbs, and sauté until the crumbs are lightly golden, 1 to 2 minutes. Use a strainer-skimmer to transfer the bread crumbs to a small bowl and set aside.

2. Pour another ¼ cup of the olive oil into the pan, and cook the onion over medium heat until dark golden brown, 5 to 7 minutes. Add the lemon zest toward the end of the cooking time. Remove the onions to a medium bowl and set aside.

3. Pour the remaining ¼ cup olive oil into the pan and, over high heat, cook the zucchini until golden on all sides, about 5 minutes. Toward the end, add the sliced garlic. Remove from the heat.

4. Using a strainer-skimmer, place the zucchini and in the dish with the onions, season with salt and pepper to taste, and cover to keep warm.

5. Meanwhile, in a large pot, bring water seasoned with salt to a boil, and cook the pasta for 6 to 8 minutes, or until al dente.

6. Drain the pasta, then toss in the pasta pot with the zucchini and onions. Sprinkle with the toasted bread crumbs before serving.

Bucatini alla Amatriciana

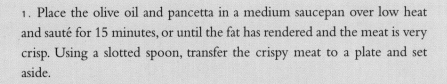

4 TO 6 SERVINGS

1/4 cup extra-virgin olive oil

8 ounces pancetta, prosciutto, or
   guanciale, cut into 1/2-inch cubes

1 1/2 pounds very ripe tomatoes or 1 1/2
   pounds canned imported Italian
   tomatoes, drained

1 medium red onion, thinly sliced

3 garlic cloves, peeled and crushed
   with knife

1 tablespoon red pepper flakes

Salt and freshly ground black pepper

1 tablespoon fresh or dried Greek oregano

2 pounds uncooked bucatini or large
   rigatoni

1/2 cup grated Pecorino Romano or
   Parmigiano cheese

1. Place the olive oil and pancetta in a medium saucepan over low heat and sauté for 15 minutes, or until the fat has rendered and the meat is very crisp. Using a slotted spoon, transfer the crispy meat to a plate and set aside.

2. Pass the fresh or canned tomatoes through a food mill into a bowl, using the largest disc with the largest holes.

3. Add the onion to the saucepan and sauté over medium-low heat for 5 minutes, then add the garlic, making sure the onions and garlic do not brown or burn. Once they are soft, add the tomatoes, pepper flakes, salt and pepper to taste, and oregano. Simmer for 30 minutes, or until the sauce thickens.

4. Bring a large pot of salted water to a boil. Cook the pasta until al dente, 9 to 12 minutes.

5. Add the reserved meat to the sauce and cook for 10 minutes over low heat. Remove the skillet from the heat and add the cheese, mixing well. Drain the pasta and toss thoroughly with the sauce.

Pappardelle with Duck Ragu

⁂

4 TO 6 SERVINGS

¹/₄ cup extra-virgin olive oil
1 pound boneless, skinless duck meat,
    cut into ¹/₂-inch cubes
Salt and freshly ground black pepper
1 onion, finely chopped
1 large carrot, finely chopped
1 stalk celery, finely chopped
4 garlic cloves, thinly sliced
One 6-ounce can tomato paste
2 cups dry red wine
2 cups brown chicken, duck, or veal stock
1 tablespoon roughly chopped fresh
    rosemary
1 pound uncooked fresh or dry
    pappardelle
¹/₄ cup freshly grated Parmesan or
    Asiago cheese

1. In a 6- to 8-quart, heavy bottomed casserole, saucepan, or Dutch oven, heat the olive oil over high heat, until it is just smoking. Season the duck with salt and pepper to taste, and sear the pieces of duck in several batches until it is evenly browned, 1 to 2 minutes. Remove all the browned meat and set aside on a plate.

2. In the same pan, add the onion, carrot, celery, and garlic. Stirring constantly with a wooden spoon, cook for 5 to 7 minutes until lightly browned. Add the tomato paste and stir to work in thoroughly. Cook until the tomato paste is lightly browned, 3 to 4 minutes. Add the wine, stock, and rosemary and bring the mixture to a boil. Return the browned duck meat to the pot, bring the liquid to a boil, reduce the heat to a simmer, and cook, uncovered, until the meat is tender and almost falling apart, about 1 hour. The sauce should have a thick, rich consistency. Adjust the seasoning to taste. Remove the sauce from the heat, cover, and keep hot.

3. In a large pot, bring 6 quarts of water to a boil, season with salt, and add the pappardelle. Cook the pasta until it begins to float, 1 to 2 minutes at most, and drain well. Add the pappardelle to the pan with the ragu and toss well but very gently. Transfer the pasta to a platter or large bowl. Add grated cheese to the top of the pasta and serve.

Penne Gratin

❧❧

1 pound uncooked penne pasta
Salt
1 cup diced prosciutto
3 tablespoons olive oil
$^1/_2$ cup unsalted butter
1 cup heavy cream
4 $^1/_2$ cups grated Parmesan cheese
$^1/_2$ cup diced fontina cheese
$^1/_2$ cup diced fresh mozzarella
Freshly ground black pepper

1. Bring a large pot of lightly salted water to a boil. Cook the pasta until al dente, 8 to 10 minutes. Drain and keep warm.

2. Meanwhile, in a sauté pan over low heat, sauté the prosciutto in the olive oil for about 3 minutes, or until the prosciutto is wilted.

3. Preheat the broiler. In a sauté pan over medium heat, melt the butter. Add the prosciutto, heavy cream, 3½ cups of the Parmesan cheese, the fontina, mozzarella, and a pinch of pepper. Bring the sauce to a light boil, add the pasta, toss, and transfer the pasta to a shallow baking dish.

4. Sprinkle the remaining 1 cup of Parmesan cheese on top of the pasta and broil for 5 to 6 minutes, or until golden brown.

Penne with Veal and Chicken Bolognese

4 SERVINGS

1 medium onion, coarsely chopped
1 large bulb fennel, coarsely chopped
1 large carrot, coarsely chopped
1/2 cup olive oil
1 teaspoon crushed red pepper flakes
3 large garlic cloves, finely chopped
1 pound ground chicken
1 pound ground veal
2 cups tomato puree
1 cup white wine
2 cups veal stock
Salt and freshly ground black pepper
1 pound uncooked penne pasta
1/4 cup butter
Parmesan cheese

1. In a food processor, grind the onion, fennel, and carrot until fine.

2. In a large saucepan, heat the olive oil over low heat. Add the ground vegetables, pepper flakes, and garlic and simmer for about 30 minutes, or until the moisture evaporates, stirring occasionally.

3. Add the ground chicken, veal, tomato puree, wine, and stock to the saucepan. Stir to mix and simmer over medium-low heat, stirring occasionally, for 1½ hours or until the sauce thickens and is reduced by one quarter. Season to taste with salt and pepper.

4. Bring a large pot of lightly salted water to a boil and cook the pasta for 6 to 8 minutes, until al dente.

5. Drain the pasta and add it to the sauce. Stir in the butter and sprinkle with Parmesan cheese to serve.

Fusilli with Roasted Tomatoes, Seasonal Mushrooms, Spinach, Garlic, and Extra-Virgin Olive Oil

❧

4 TO 6 SERVINGS

FOR THE ROASTED TOMATOES (MAKES 2 CUPS):

1 pound ripe Roma tomatoes, cut in half lengthwise
1 tablespoon extra-virgin olive oil
Salt and freshly ground black pepper

FOR THE SAUCE:

4 tablespoons extra-virgin olive oil
3 garlic cloves, thinly sliced
2 cups sliced or quartered mushrooms (a combination of shiitake, oyster, cremini, and portobello)
3 cups fresh spinach, stems removed
1/2 cup mushroom or vegetable broth*
Salt and freshly ground black pepper
1 pound uncooked farro fusilli, penne, or rigatoni
Freshly grated Parmesan or Pecorino Romano cheese

1. TO MAKE THE ROASTED TOMATOES: Preheat the oven to 225°F. Lightly squeeze out the seeds and remove the insides of the tomatoes. In a medium bowl, toss the tomatoes with the olive oil and salt and pepper to taste, until they are evenly coated.

2. Place the tomatoes cut side down on a baking sheet lined with parchment paper. Roast for 4 to 5 hours, or until the tomatoes are soft and have lost their liquid. They should look slightly darker and shriveled, and have a very intense favor. Store in the refrigerator covered with extra-virgin olive oil for up to 5 days.

3. TO MAKE THE SAUCE: In a 12- to 14-inch sauté pan, combine the olive oil and garlic, and sauté until garlic is almost light brown, about 2 minutes. Add the mushrooms and saute until their moisture has evaporated and they turn brown, about 2 minutes more. If necessary, add 1 to 2 tablespoons more olive oil. Once the mushrooms are evenly browned, add 1 cup of the roasted tomatoes and the spinach. Moisten the sauté pan with the broth and toss thoroughly. Season with salt and pepper.

4. Bring 6 quarts of water seasoned with salt to a boil. Cook the pasta until al dente**, drain, and add the pasta to the prepared sauce and toss thoroughly. Top the pasta with the cheese.

*NOTE: *The broth can be easily made by simmering the mushroom stems and trimmings with 1 can vegetable, chicken, or beef broth for 20 minutes. Then strain the broth through a fine sieve to remove the stems.*

**NOTE: *Farro pasta is made from ground spelt, a form of wild barley grain, which will require more cooking time than normal pasta, so make sure to read the manufacturer's cooking directions.*

Cheese Lasagna

≋

8 SERVINGS

2 pounds fresh mozzarella, diced

2 cups grated Parmigiano Reggiano cheese

5 pounds fresh ricotta cheese

3 eggs

1/2 cup chopped fresh parsley

Salt and freshly ground black pepper

4 uncooked fresh pasta sheets (store-bought), or 2 pounds uncooked lasagna noodles

6 cups tomato sauce (double recipe on page 100)

1. In a large bowl, mix ¾ of the mozzarella, 1 cup of the Parmigiano Reggiano, and the ricotta. Stir in the eggs and parsley. Season with salt and pepper to taste and set aside.

2. Bring a large pot of salted water to a boil over high heat and cook the pasta until almost al dente, about 1 minute for fresh pasta and 6 to 8 for dried. Drain and shock in cold water. Remove the pasta from the water and set aside.

3. In a large saucepan, heat the tomato sauce over low heat.

4. Preheat the oven to 350°F. Pour 1 cup of the hot tomato sauce in the bottom of an 8 × 12-inch baking pan. Place a pasta sheet or a few lasagna noodles over the layer of sauce, cutting the sheet to fit if necessary.

5. Spread ⅓ of the ricotta mixture over the pasta. Add some of the sauce and sprinkle with some of the remaining mozzarella and Parmesan. Repeat the layers of sauce, pasta, and cheeses two more times, finishing with pasta on top.

6. Spread the remaining cup of tomato sauce over the top layer of the pasta and sprinkle the remaining Parmigiano Reggiano cheese over the sauce.

7. Bake the lasagna for 1 hour, or until the top is golden.

Cavatelli with Sweet Italian Sausage and Broccoli Rabe

୧୨

4 TO 6 SERVINGS

4 tablespoons extra-virgin olive oil

1 medium onion, cut into small dice

3 garlic cloves, thinly sliced

12 ounces coarsely ground sweet fennel
    sausage, casings removed

1 bunch broccoli rabe, tender tops and
    tender stems only, cut into 3- to 4-inch
    pieces

1 teaspoon red pepper flakes

1/2 cup chicken broth

1 pound uncooked fresh or frozen cavatelli

6 tablespoons freshly grated Parmesan

1. In a heavy saucepan over medium heat, heat the olive oil. Add the onion and garlic and sauté for 10 minutes, but do not brown. Remove the onion and garlic from the pan and set aside. In the same pan, add the sausage and sauté for 10 to 15 minutes, or until lightly browned. Add the broccoli rabe and broth and sauté until it is soft but still green and firm, about 8 minutes. Add in the onion, garlic, and pepper flakes and simmer for 5 to 10 minutes longer, or until the broccoli rabe is done to taste.

2. Meanwhile, bring a large pot of salted water to a boil. Cook the cavatelli according to package directions, for 3 to 4 minutes. Strain the pasta and toss with the sauce. As you are tossing the cavatelli, add the Parmesan cheese until it is completely mixed.

Penne with Fresh Tomato Sauce

୧୨

6 SERVINGS

1/2 cup extra-virgin olive oil

3 garlic gloves, minced

2 pounds ripe tomatoes, peeled, seeded,
    and chopped

1/4 to 1 teaspoon crushed hot red pepper
    flakes

1 teaspoon salt

8 fresh basil leaves, finely shredded

1 pound uncooked penne pasta

2 tablespoons unsalted butter, at room
    temperature

Freshly grated Parmigiano Reggiano
    cheese

1. In a large saucepan over medium heat, heat the olive oil. Add the garlic and cook, stirring, for 3 minutes, or until the garlic just begins to turn golden brown. Increase the heat to medium-high, add the tomatoes, red pepper flakes, and salt, and cook, stirring occasionally, for 15 minutes, or until the tomatoes are softened and a sauce is formed. Stir in the basil.

2. Meanwhile, cook the pasta in a large pot of boiling, salted water until al dente, about one minute less than the package directions. Drain the pasta in a colander, reserving 1 cup of the cooking water.

3. Return the pasta to the cooking pot and add the sauce. Add the reserved cooking water and cook, stirring, over medium-high heat for 2 minutes, or until the sauce adheres to the pasta. Stir in the butter. Arrange the pasta in a serving bowl and top with the Parmigiano Reggiano.

Pasta e Fagioli

1 pound dried white beans, such as cannellini or navy, rinsed and picked over
1/2 cup olive oil
1 tablespoon chopped garlic
1 large onion, coarsely chopped (about
  1 1/2 cups)
1/4 pound prosciutto (in one piece)
1/4 teaspoon crushed red pepper flakes, or
  to taste
1 cup canned Italian plum tomatoes
1/4 teaspoon salt
1 pound uncooked tubettini pasta
3/4 cup freshly grated Parmesan cheese
Freshly ground black pepper

1. Put the beans in a large pot and add enough cold water to cover them by 3 to 4 inches. Set aside to soak overnight. Drain and rinse the beans with fresh water. Cover the beans with water and boil for 1 ½ hours over medium-low heat. Drain.

2. In a large pot, heat the oil over medium heat. Add the garlic, onions, and prosciutto and cook for 2 to 3 minutes, or until the onions are soft and golden. Add the pepper flakes and tomatoes and cook, uncovered, for 10 minutes, or until the tomatoes are cooked down.

3. Add the beans and bring the mixture to a boil over medium-high heat. Reduce the heat to a simmer and cook, uncovered, for 30 minutes, or until the beans are very tender.

4. In a large pot of lightly salted boiling water, cook the pasta for 8 to 10 minutes, or until al dente. Drain.

5. Add the pasta to the beans and stir over high heat for 1 ½ to 2 minutes to allow the pasta to combine with the sauce.

6. Garnish generously with grated cheese (about 2 tablespoons per serving) and pepper and serve.

Meatball Lasagna

∾

6 SERVINGS

FOR THE MEATBALLS:

2 slices white bread

1/2 cup milk

2 pounds ground beef

1 cup finely chopped onions

3 tablespoons chopped fresh parsley

2 eggs

4 tablespoons grated Parmesan cheese

1 1/2 tablespoons chopped garlic

Salt and freshly ground black pepper

3 tablespoons olive oil

5 cups tomato sauce (double recipe on page 100)

FOR THE LASAGNA:

2 pounds fresh mozzarella, diced

2 cups grated Parmigiano Reggiano cheese

5 pounds fresh ricotta cheese

3 eggs

1/2 cup chopped fresh flat-leaf parsley

Salt and freshly ground black pepper

4 uncooked fresh pasta sheets (store-bought), or 2 pounds uncooked lasagna noodles

1. TO MAKE THE MEATBALLS: In a bowl, soak the bread in the milk. In a medium bowl, mix the ground beef, bread and milk, onions, parsley, eggs, cheese, and garlic. Add salt and pepper to taste. If the mixture is dry, add 1/2 cup of cold water and mix well. Form the mixture into about 12 meatballs.

2. Place the meatballs and the olive oil in a sauté pan and fry over medium to high heat until brown, 10 to 15 minutes, turning them regularly. Dry the meatballs on paper towels.

3. In a stockpot, bring the tomato sauce to a simmer over low heat. Add the meatballs to the sauce and cover. Simmer for 30 minutes, or until the meatballs are cooked through. Remove from the heat and set aside.

4. **TO MAKE THE LASAGNA:** Mix three-quarters of the mozzarella, 1 cup of the Parmigiano Reggiano, and the ricotta in a large bowl. Add the eggs and parsley. Season with salt and pepper to taste and set aside.

5. Remove the meatballs from the sauce. Crumble the meatballs and set aside.

6. Bring a large pot of salted water to a boil over high heat and cook the pasta until al dente, about 1 minute for the fresh pasta or 8 to 10 minutes for the dried pasta. Drain and shock in cold water.

7. **TO ASSEMBLE:** Preheat the oven to 350°F. Pour 1 cup of the hot tomato sauce in the bottom of an 8 × 12-inch baking pan. Place a pasta sheet over the layer of sauce, cutting the sheet of fit if necessary.

8. Spread ⅓ of the ricotta mixture over the pasta. Spread ⅓ of the crumbled meatballs over the cheese. Add some of the sauce and sprinkle with the remaining mozzarella and some Parmesan. Repeat the layers of sauce, pasta, cheese, and meatballs two more times, finishing with pasta on top.

9. Spread the remaining cup of tomato sauce over the top layer of the pasta and sprinkle the remaining Parmigiano Reggiano cheese over the sauce.

10. Bake the lasagna for 1 hour, or until the top is golden.

Pasta Al Forno with Tomatoes and Basil

❧

6 SERVINGS

FOR THE BREAD CRUMBS:

2 cups prepackaged bread crumbs
1/2 cup olive oil
1 tablespoon chopped garlic
1/2 cup chopped fresh basil
Salt and freshly ground black pepper

FOR THE PASTA AL FORNO:

3 pounds fresh plum tomatoes
1/2 cup extra-virgin olive oil
1 tablespoon chopped garlic
1 cup chopped fresh basil
Salt and freshly ground black pepper
1 pound uncooked tubettini pasta
1/2 cup butter, cut into small pieces
2 cups freshly grated Parmesan cheese

1. **TO MAKE THE BREAD CRUMBS:** Preheat the oven to 250°F. Spread the bread crumbs on a baking sheet and toast until they are golden brown, about 5 minutes.

2. In a small pan over medium heat, sauté the olive oil, garlic, and basil until the garlic is golden brown, about 2 minutes. Add the salt and pepper to taste. Let the mixture cool to room temperature, then mix with the bread crumbs.

3. **TO MAKE THE PASTA AL FORNO:** Raise the oven temperature to 300°F. In a medium sauce pan of boiling water, blanch the whole tomatoes for 1 minute, then cool the tomatoes in a bowl of ice water. Peel the tomatoes, cut them in half, remove the seeds, and dice. Heat the olive oil in a pan and sauté the garlic until golden brown, about 2 minutes. Add the tomatoes, the basil, and salt and pepper to taste and simmer until cooked through and the tomatoes break down, 5 to 7 minutes.

4. Meanwhile, bring a large pot of salted water to a boil over high heat and cook the pasta until almost al dente, about 5 to 7 minutes; drain well.

5. In a sauté pan, combine the butter, pasta, and 1 cup of the Parmesan cheese. Add salt and pepper to taste.

6. In a buttered 12 × 6-inch gratin dish, place the pasta on the bottom, then add the tomatoes, and top with the toasted bread crumbs and sprinkle with the remaining 1 cup Parmesan and the butter.

7. Bake until the crust is dark and golden, about 15 minutes.

Garganelli with Rock Shrimp, Zucchini, and Toasted Bread Crumbs

1/4 cup extra-virgin olive oil

2 medium zucchini, cut in half lengthwise, then bias-cut 1/4 inch thick

3 garlic cloves, thinly sliced

1 pound rock shrimp, peeled and deveined

Salt

1 pound uncooked dry or fresh garganelli

Freshly ground black pepper

3 tablespoons roughly chopped fresh basil

1/2 cup freshly toasted bread crumbs (see page 106).

1. In a large sauté pan, heat the olive oil over medium heat. Add the zucchini and cook until light brown and firm, about 5 minutes. Add the garlic and sauté until lightly browned, 2 minutes more. Add the rock shrimp and cook for 2 to 3 minutes, or until they are pink. Set aside.

2. Bring a large pot of water to a boil and season with salt. Cook the garganelli according to directions; for dry pasta cook 5 to 6 minutes, and for fresh pasta, 2 to 3 minutes. Drain the pasta and toss with the zucchini and shrimp. Season with salt and pepper to taste and fold in the basil. Just before serving, top the pasta with the bread crumbs.

NOTE: *The sauce should be made very quickly so that the zucchini and shrimp do not overcook. It is important to brown the zucchini to bring out its natural sweet flavor, which will complement the shrimps' flavor.*

Fettuccine with Pesto Sauce, String Beans, Yukon Gold Potatoes, and Marigold Petals

6 SERVINGS

**FOR THE BASIL PESTO
(MAKES ABOUT 4 CUPS):**

¹/2 cup pine nuts
4 cups basil leaves, washed and dried in
    a salad spinner
3 cloves garlic, crushed
Juice of ¹/2 lemon
1 cup extra-virgin olive oil
¹/2 cup freshly grated Parmesan cheese
Salt and freshly ground black pepper

FOR THE FETTUCCINE:

¹/2 pound string beans, cut in half
1 pound Yukon gold potatoes, diced small
¹/4 cup extra-virgin olive oil
1 tablespoon chopped garlic
¹/2 tablespoon julienned shallots
Salt
2 pounds uncooked fresh fettuccine
Freshly ground black pepper
4 ounces fresh marigold petals

1. **TO MAKE THE BASIL PESTO:** In a hot sauté pan, toss the pine nuts for 2 minutes or until golden. Remove the pine nuts from the heat and set aside.

2. Place the basil, garlic, and lemon juice in a food processor and process until well combined. With the machine running, drizzle in the olive oil. Add the pine nuts and Parmesan and process briefly to retain some texture in the pesto.

3. Season with salt and pepper to taste.

4. **TO MAKE THE FETTUCCINE:** Place the string beans and potatoes in boiling water for 1 minute. Place them in a cool bath, then carefully remove them with a slotted spoon. Drain and let cool on a paper towel.

5. In a large pan, heat the oil and sauté the garlic and shallots over medium to high heat for 2 to 3 minutes, until golden brown. Add the string beans and potatoes and sauté for 1 minute, or until warmed through.

6. In a large pot of lightly salted boiling water, cook the fettuccine for 3 minutes or until al dente. Drain the pasta and add it to the sauté pan with the string beans and potatoes.

7. Simmer for about 2 minutes over medium heat, then add ⅓ cup of the basil pesto and toss. Make sure there is pesto throughout the dish. Season with salt and pepper to taste, garnish with the marigold petals, and serve.

NOTE: *Leftover pesto can be frozen for up to 2 months.*

Pumpkin Gnocchi with Grated Amaretti Cookies

⌘

6 SERVINGS

8 ounces cheese pumpkin or butternut
   squash, peeled, seeded, and cut into
   2-inch pieces
Salt and freshly ground black pepper
Sugar
3 pounds russet potatoes
2 1/2 cups all-purpose flour
1 extra-large egg
1 teaspoon salt
1 cup extra-virgin olive oil
3 tablespoons butter
3 small amaretti cookies
1/2 cup grated Parmigiano Reggiano

1. Preheat the oven to 300°F. Season the pumpkin with salt, pepper, and sugar to taste and wrap well in aluminum foil. Roast for 1 hour. Unwrap and transfer the cooked pumpkin flesh, less any excess juice, to a food processor and puree until smooth. Let cool.

2. Meanwhile, place the potatoes in a saucepan with water to cover. Cook at a low boil until soft, about 45 minutes. While the potatoes are still warm, peel them and pass them through a food mill or ricer. Do not mash.

3. Place the potatoes on a clean work surface. Make a well in the center of the potatoes and fold in the pumpkin puree until it is evenly incorporated. Create another well and sprinkle the flour all over the pumpkin and potatoes. Break the egg in the center, add the salt, and mix together with a fork, as you would for pasta dough. When the egg is mixed in, bring the dough together and knead into a ball form. Continue to knead for 2 to 3 minutes, or until the ball is dry to the touch.

4. Bring 7 quarts of water to a boil in a large pot.

5. Divide the dough into 4 balls. Roll one ball at a time into a ¾-inch rope and cut it into ¾-inch pieces. Drop the dough pieces into the boiling water and cook until the pieces float to the surface, about 3 minutes. Use a skimmer or slotted spoon to remove the gnocchi and transfer them into an ice water bath. Continue making and cooking the gnocchi until the dough is gone. Remove the gnocchi from the ice bath, drain, and add to a mixing bowl. Toss with a little olive oil and set aside until ready to cook.

6. Heat the butter and olive oil in a frying pan over medium-high heat and fry the gnocchi until they are golden brown, about 3 minutes. Season the gnocchi with salt and pepper to taste. Place the gnocchi in a bowl or on a plate. Using a hand grater, grate the amaretti cookies over the gnocchi and sprinkle with Parmigiano.

Cheddar Cheese Risotto with Caramelized Onions
and Smoked Ham

❧

6 SERVINGS

2 quarts chicken or vegetable stock
4 tablespoons unsalted butter
3 large onions, cut into small dice
2 stalks celery, cut into small dice
2 garlic cloves, minced
1 pound arborio rice
1 cup smoked country ham, cut into small cubes
1 tablespoon fresh thyme leaves
1/2 cup dry white wine
3/4 pound Vermont cheddar, shredded
Salt and freshly ground black pepper

1. In a large pot over medium heat, heat the stock until simmering.

2. In a large sauté pan, heat 1 tablespoon of the butter over high heat. Add the onions and celery and cook 5 to 7 minutes until caramelized, being careful not to burn the vegetables. Add the garlic and cook for 1 minute. Add the rice and sauté while stirring with a wooden spoon for 5 to 7 minutes over low heat. When the rice begins to stick to the bottom, add the ham and thyme and continue to stir.

3. Add the wine and cook, stirring, for 2 minutes, or until it is nearly absorbed.

4. Ladle about 1 cup of the hot stock into the rice. Cook for about 2 minutes, stirring often, until the stock is almost completely absorbed. Continue to add more stock 1 cup at a time, stirring gently until the broth is absorbed by the rice before adding the next cup.

5. After about 15 minutes, begin tasting the rice. At this point, add the stock with caution. The rice should be firm, yet cooked through. The entire process will take 18 to 20 minutes.

6. Stir in all but 4 tablespoons of the cheddar cheese and the remaining 3 tablespoons of butter. Season with salt and pepper to taste. Garnish with the remaining 4 tablespoons cheese and serve.

Risotto with Roasted Red Peppers,
Trevisano, and Pancetta

4 SERVINGS

FOR THE RED PEPPER PUREE:

4 red bell peppers
1/4 cup extra-virgin olive oil
1/2 cup chicken stock
Salt and freshly ground black pepper

FOR THE RISOTTO:

5 cups chicken stock
6 tablespoons extra-virgin olive oil
1 tablespoon chopped garlic
1/2 pound carnaroli rice
1/2 cup white wine
1/2 cup grated Parmesan cheese
Salt and freshly ground black pepper

FOR THE TREVISANO SALAD:

1/4 pound pancetta, diced
2 tablespoons extra-virgin olive oil
2 heads Trevisano lettuce (or radicchio)

1. TO MAKE THE RED PEPPER PUREE: Preheat the oven to 350°F. Rub the peppers with the oil, place on a baking sheet, and roast for about 20 minutes or until skin is blackened. As soon as the peppers are done roasting, place them in a bowl and cover it with plastic wrap. Allow the peppers to cool, then peel off the skin.

2. In a blender, add the peppers, chicken stock, and salt and pepper to taste and blend until smooth. Set aside.

3. TO MAKE THE RISOTTO: Meanwhile, in a medium saucepan, simmer the stock over low heat.

4. In a large heavy stockpot, heat the olive oil over medium heat. Add the garlic and cook for 3 to 5 minutes, until golden brown. Using a slotted spoon, remove the garlic from the oil and discard the garlic.

5. Raise the heat to medium-high, add the rice to the oil, and stir for about 15 seconds, or until the grains are well coated with oil.

6. Add the wine to the rice and stir constantly, being careful to scrape the sides and bottom of the pan gently so that the rice does not stick. When the wine is almost gone, add ½ cup of the hot stock and stir until the stock is nearly absorbed by the rice. Repeat, adding ½ cup of the stock at a time, until all the stock is used. The entire process will take 17 to 18 minutes. It is very important to stir the rice constantly for even cooking and a creamy texture, although it will remain al dente.

7. Mix the red pepper puree in with the finished risotto.

8. **TO MAKE THE TREVISANO SALAD:** In a medium sauté pan over medium heat, sauté the pancetta in olive oil until crispy.

9. Separate the leaves of Trevisano and add with the pancetta in a mixing bowl. Toss, and top with the risotto. Sprinkle with the Parmesan and season with salt and pepper to taste.

Risotto with Snap Peas, Fava Beans, String Beans, Crisp Prosciutto, and Shaved Parmesan

❦

4 SERVINGS

12 slices prosciutto
4 cups chicken stock
2 tablespoons extra-virgin olive oil, plus
    additional for garnish
2 ¹/₂ tablespoons unsalted butter
4 shallots, diced
2 garlic cloves, finely chopped
1 ¹/₂ cups arborio rice
¹/₂ cup freshly grated Parmesan
¹/₄ cup pesto (recipe on page 109)
¹/₂ pound shelled snap peas, blanched
2 cups shelled fava beans, blanched
¹/₂ pound fresh string beans, blanched
Salt and freshly ground black pepper
Shaved Parmesan cheese

1. Preheat the oven to 200°F. Lay the prosciutto in a single layer on a baking sheet and bake until crisp 3 to 5 minutes. Set aside.

2. In a large pot, heat the chicken stock over medium heat until simmering.

3. In a heavy saucepan over low heat heat the olive oil and 1¼ tablespoons of the butter. Add the shallots and garlic to the oil and gently sauté until the shallots are transparent, about 2 minutes. Add the rice and stir until the rice is well coated with oil.

4. Reduce the heat to low, add 1 cup of the boiling chicken stock, and stir briefly. Allow the risotto to cook and the stock to be almost completely absorbed by the rice before adding another 1 cup stock, then stir again. Continue adding stock and cooking, stirring frequently, until the rice is tender and creamy, 15 to 20 minutes. You may not need all the stock.

5. Stir in the grated Parmesan, remaining 1¼ tablespoons butter, and the pesto. Stir in the snap peas, fava beans, and string beans. Season with salt and pepper to taste.

6. To serve, spoon the risotto into wide shallow bowls and top it with shaved Parmesan, the crisped prosciutto, a splash of olive oil, and some pepper.

When Mom/Marion was growing up, there were plenty of vegetarians. Of course, you could sum them up in five words: Jack La Lanne, nudists, and Communists. Or that's what most red-meat-eating Americans thought they (that would be "vegetarians") were. Of course that was then and this is now—and now there's a good chance that a quarter of your Sunday guests will be nonmeat-eating grass eaters. Oooops. Sorry. It's just that Italian-Americans—people who literally grew up not only with, but *because* of meatballs—often find the concept of all veggies all the time well, different. (That's not to say, however, that man cannot live by risotto, pizza, or pasta alone!)

Some of our best friends are vegetarians, and because we love the veggie eaters like we love the meatball eaters, we now prepare Sunday dinner with those friends in mind, too. (Never forget that the worst thing that can happen to an Italian-American, short of missing his or her own mother's birthday, is to serve a dinner without something for everyone!)

Those fears aside, it's always good, prudent, and just plain wise to have one side veggie dish large and hearty enough to double as an entrée in case you have vegetarian guests. Our Eggplant and Zucchini Pie, for example, is a meal in itself. Best of all, it can be made the day before you serve. In fact, you *should* make it the day before. Eggplant and Zucchini Pie—like a great love affair—actually seems even better the next day.

Here, then, are veggie dishes so good, you'd think they were made of, well, meatballs.

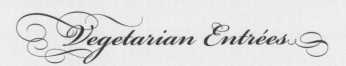

Vegetarian Entrées

Creamy Polenta with Wild Spring Mushrooms, Fontina, and Mozzarella

4 TO 6 SERVINGS

3 cups whole milk

1 cup water

1 cup instant polenta

1/2 cup mascarpone

2 tablespoons plus 1/4 cup olive oil

1 1/2 pounds any variety fresh wild mushrooms* (morels, chanterelles, hen of the woods, black trumpet, lobster), cleaned, soaked in cold water, and drained

3 garlic cloves, thinly sliced

1 sprig fresh rosemary, leaves roughly chopped

Salt and freshly ground black pepper

4 tablespoons butter

1/2 cup fresh mozzarella, cut into 1/4-inch cubes

1/2 cup fresh fontina, cut into 1/4-inch cubes

1/2 cup grated Parmigiano-Reggiano

6 sprigs fresh flat-leaf parsley, leaves roughly chopped

1. In a large pot over medium heat, bring the milk and water to a simmer. Do not scald. While it is simmering, slowly pour in the polenta. Stir constantly for 6 to 7 minutes, or until the liquid has been absorbed.

2. Remove the pot from the heat and stir in the mascarpone. Set the polenta aside.

3. In a 10-inch sauté pan over high heat, heat 2 tablespoons of the olive oil until it is lightly smoking, then add the mushrooms in two batches.

Sauté the mushrooms until light brown and tender. Remove the pan from the heat and place the mushrooms in a medium bowl. While the sauté pan is still hot, add the remaining ¼ cup olive oil and sauté the garlic until light brown, about 2 minutes. Remove the pan from the heat and add the rosemary. Pour the mixture over the mushrooms. Season with salt and pepper to taste.

4. Preheat the broiler to its highest setting.

5. Lightly butter six 5-inch gratin dishes and set aside.

6. Place the pot of polenta on low heat and add the mozzarella, fontina, and wild mushroom ragu.

7. Spoon equal amounts of the polenta into each gratin dish, but do not overfill. Sprinkle the polenta with Parmigiano cheese. Place the dishes on the upper shelf of the broiler and broil until the cheese is light brown and the polenta is crusty, 1 to 2 minutes.

8. Sprinkle the polenta with the parsley and serve.

*NOTE: *If wild mushrooms are not available, the store variety of shiitake, oyster, or portobello make great substitutes. If using shiitake mushrooms, remove the stems completely, as they are inedible. The black gills on the underside of portobello mushrooms can be removed by scraping with a spoon. For oyster mushrooms, discard the bottom part of the stem.*

Eggplant and Zucchini Pie

❧

6 SERVINGS

FOR THE CHEESE MIXTURE:

2 pounds fresh ricotta cheese
2 pounds fresh mozzarella cheese, diced
1 cup grated Parmesan cheese
1/4 cup chopped fresh parsley
4 eggs
Salt and freshly ground black pepper

FOR THE EGGPLANT AND ZUCCHINI PIE:

2 medium eggplants, peeled
4 medium zucchini
Salt
4 cups all-purpose flour
10 eggs
4 cups prepackaged bread crumbs
2 cups grated Parmesan cheese
1/4 cup chopped fresh flat-leaf parsley
Freshly ground black pepper
2 quarts olive oil or vegetable cooking oil
5 cups tomato sauce (see page 100)

1. **TO MAKE THE CHEESE MIXTURE:** In a large bowl, combine the ricotta, mozzarella, Parmesan, parsley, and eggs. Mix well and season with salt and pepper to taste. Refrigerate briefly to firm the mixture.

2. **TO MAKE THE EGGPLANT AND ZUCCHINI PIE:** Slice the eggplants and zucchini into 1/4-inch-thick round slices. Set the zucchini aside. Fill a bowl with lightly salted water, add the eggplants, and soak for 1 1/2 to 2 hours to remove the bitter taste. Drain.

3. In one shallow bowl, place the flour. In a second bowl, beat the eggs with a fork until blended. In a third bowl, mix the bread crumbs, 1 1/2 cups of the Parmesan cheese, the parsley, and salt and pepper to taste. Line up the bowls on a work surface.

4. One at a time, carefully dip the eggplant and zucchini slices first into the flour, making sure both sides are covered; then into the egg mixture, and finally into the bread crumb mixture. Coat both sides very well and gently tap off any excess coating. Transfer the eggplant and zucchini slices to a large plate and season with salt and pepper to taste.

5. In a large, heavy skillet over medium heat, heat the olive oil. Add the eggplant slices in a single layer and sauté on both sides until golden brown, about 3 minutes on each side, making sure that they are soft and cooked all the way through. Try not to crowd the pan. Fry the zucchini next. Place the cooked eggplant and zucchini on paper towels to drain off the excess oil.

6. Preheat the oven to 450°F. In a 9 × 13-inch baking pan, spread 1 cup of the tomato sauce, then a layer of 1/4 of the eggplant and zucchini, and top with a layer of 1/4 of the cheese mixture. Repeat the process three times. Top with a layer of tomato sauce and sprinkle with the remaining 1/2 cup Parmesan cheese.

7. Bake for 20 minutes, or until golden brown.

Sweet Potato–Stuffed Pumpkins

❧

4 SERVINGS

FOR THE PUMPKINS:

4 small pumpkins
1/2 cup butter
1 tablespoon brown sugar
1/2 tablespoon honey

FOR THE SWEET POTATO PUREE:

1/2 cup butter
1 cup chopped shallots
4 pounds sweet potatoes
2 cups heavy cream
1 tablespoon brown sugar
2 teaspoons salt
2 teaspoons freshly ground black pepper

1. **TO MAKE THE PUMPKINS:** Preheat the oven to 325°F. Remove the tops from the pumpkins and reserve and spoon out the seeds. In a small bowl, combine the butter, brown sugar, and honey. Coat the inside of the pumpkins with the butter. Bake for 10 minutes, or until the pumpkins soften.

2. **TO MAKE THE SWEET POTATO PUREE:** Meanwhile, peel the sweet potatoes, cut them into small chunks, and boil them in water to cover until tender, about 15 minutes. Drain and set aside. In a 3-quart pot over medium heat, melt the butter, add the shallots and sauté until tender and translucent, 2 to 3 minutes. Add the potatoes, cream, sugar, salt, and pepper and blend with a fork until smooth. Simmer over low heat for 10 minutes.

3. Fill each pumpkin with the sweet potato puree and bake for 4 to 6 minutes, or until the pumpkin flesh is tender and golden brown. Top with the reserved pumpkin "hat."

Love Tart with Herb Goat Cheese, Roasted Plum Tomatoes, and Red Peppers

❧

6 SERVINGS

FOR THE TART CRUST:

1 cup flour
1 teaspoon salt
1/2 cup shortening
4 tablespoons cold water

FOR THE ROASTED PLUM TOMATOES AND PEPPERS:

4 plum tomatoes, halved
2 to 3 red bell peppers, halved
1 tablespoon chopped fresh thyme
1 tablespoon chopped fresh oregano
1 tablespoon chopped fresh rosemary
1/4 cup extra-virgin olive oil
Salt and freshly ground black pepper

FOR THE GOAT CHEESE FILLING:

21 ounces goat cheese
3 tablespoons grated Parmesan cheese
1/4 cup ricotta cheese
6 large eggs
1/2 cup heavy cream
4 tablespoons olive oil
1 teaspoon chopped fresh basil
1 teaspoon chopped fresh parsley
1 teaspoon chopped fresh chives
1 teaspoon chopped fresh tarragon
Salt and freshly ground black pepper

1. **TO MAKE THE TART CRUST:** Sift the flour and salt into a medium bowl and mix in 1/4 cup of the shortening until the mixture looks like cornmeal. Cut in the remaining 1/4 cup shortening until the pieces are the size of peas. Sprinkle 1 tablespoon of the water over the mixture, mix gently with a fork and push to the side of the bowl, and repeat with the remaining 3 tablespoons of water. Gather the dough and form a ball.

2. Preheat the oven and a baking sheet to 400°F. Roll out the crust on a floured surface and place it in an 8-inch round tart shell. Cut a piece of parchment paper to fit the tart shell and place it on top of the dough. Fill the shell with pie weights. Set the shell on the hot baking sheet and bake for 10 minutes. Remove the pie weights and parchment paper. Lightly prick the shell all over with a fork. Return the shell to the oven and continue baking until the crust is golden, about 10 minutes. Carefully flatten any bubbles in the shell. Cool the shell in the pan on a rack at room temperature. The tart shell can be baked up to 4 hours in advance. Cover loosely and hold at room temperature.

3. **TO MAKE THE ROASTED PLUM TOMATOES AND PEPPERS:** Preheat the oven to 300°F. On a baking sheet, place the tomatoes, peppers, chopped herbs, olive oil, and salt and pepper to taste. Roast for about 40 minutes, or until the tomatoes are almost dry. Set aside to cool.

4. **TO MAKE THE GOAT CHEESE FILLING:** Raise the oven temperature to 350°F. In a nonreactive bowl, mix the goat cheese, Parmesan, and ricotta. Let the mixture stand at room temperature until soft. Whisk in the eggs, cream, olive oil, and fresh herbs until thoroughly mixed. Season with salt and pepper to taste.

5. With a small spatula, fill the prebaked tart shell with the cheese filling. Place the roasted plum tomatoes and peppers on top of the cheese filling. Bake at 350°F for 15 to 20 minutes, or until the crust is golden and the cheese melts.

Zucchini, Sun-Dried Tomato, and Mozzarella Tart

❧

8 SERVINGS

FOR THE TART PASTRY:

2 ¼ cups unbleached all-purpose flour
1 cup unsalted butter, cut into cubes and
    chilled
1 teaspoon kosher salt
2 tablespoons water
1 large egg, lightly beaten

FOR THE TART FILLING:

2 cups shredded mozzarella cheese
½ cup plus 2 tablespoons freshly grated
    Parmesan cheese
1 cup oil-packed sun-dried tomatoes,
    drained and thinly sliced
½ cup chopped prosciutto
½ cup thinly sliced fresh basil
1 tablespoon chopped fresh oregano
2 large eggs
1 cup half-and-half
¼ teaspoon salt
¼ teaspoon freshly ground black pepper
2 small zucchini, cut into thin rounds

1. **TO MAKE THE TART PASTRY:** In a food processor fitted with the metal blade, combine the flour, butter, and salt. Pulse 9 or 10 times, until the mixture resembles coarse crumbs. Do not overmix.

2. In a small bowl, whisk together the water and egg. With the food processor running, add the egg mixture through the feeding tube. Pulse 8 to 10 times, just until the dough comes together in a cohesive mass. Do not overmix or the dough will be tough.

3. Remove the dough from the food processor and form into a ball. Flatten into a disc about 6 inches wide and 1 ½ inches thick, wrap in plastic, and refrigerate for at least 1 hour before using. Let the dough stand at room temperature for about 15 minutes before rolling out.

4. Roll out the pastry on a floured surface to a ⅛-inch-thick circle. Trim the pastry edges to form a 13-inch circle. Transfer to an 11-inch tart pan with a removable bottom. Fold in the overhang to form double-thick sides. Pierce with a fork. Cover in plastic wrap and chill for 1 hour.

5. Preheat the oven to 425°F. Line the pastry with foil. Fill the pie with beans or pie weights. Bake the pastry until the sides are set, about 20 minutes. Remove the foil and beans. Bake the crust until the bottom is golden brown, about 8 minutes. Press the pastry with the back of a fork if bubbles form. Cool for 5 minutes.

6. **TO MAKE THE TART FILLING:** Reduce the oven to 400°F. Sprinkle the mozzarella over the bottom of the crust. Top with the Parmesan cheese, tomatoes, prosciutto, basil, and oregano. Whisk the eggs, half-and-half, salt, and pepper in a medium bowl. Pour the mixture into the tart. Arrange the zucchini rounds in concentric circles to cover the top of the tart.

7. Bake the tart until custard is set and the crust is golden brown, about 40 minutes. Serve warm or at room temperature.

*A*lthough people think of pasta when they think Italian, the truth is a real Mediterranean diet is probably the healthiest (not to mention the most delicious), because it's so full of fresh veggies and even fresher fish. (The operative word here is "fresher," as in fresh, fresher, freshest!) Seriously, if we Italian-Americans didn't know how to prepare at least seven fishes, what would we eat on Christmas Eve? Take-out? No—we'd be like a fish out of water.

We really shine in the summer when we can grill fresh fish—a bit of Italy in the backyard. In fact, we Scottos love to grill fish so much we're convinced that it's the whole reason God invented barbecues. When a fish is out-of-the-water fresh, and then popped onto a very, very hot grill with some pure virgin (we're talking olive oil!) and fresh herbs,—wow!—you'd be hard-pressed to find anything as delicious, as quick to cook, or as easy to prepare.

Cooking fish this way reminds us of our trips to Italy, where fish is so fresh it needs to be slapped. In fact, some of our best memories are of lazy afternoons sitting at tiny seaside restaurants (you can't find a bad one if you tried) in Sicily eating perfectly grilled fish and sardines with a nice bottle of wine. Sicily? It's more like ordering lunch in heaven!

We try to re-create that feeling at home, too, with Sunday suppers in the summer. We often begin by even making fish *shopping* a family affair—with all the kids in tow. Of course, there's not a whole lot we Scottos don't make into a family affair. Kids at the fish market? Yes, absolutely! Crazy as it sounds, it's never too early to take the kids with you. They get a kick out of not only being able to pick out the fish, but by helping to grill "their" fish whole—just like they do in Italy—later that day.

Here then, are the tips we teach not only the kids, but any non-Scottos who come, er, fishing with us.

You need to remember only five things when picking your fish. The first is that these four tips are totally non-negotiable.

1) CHECK THE EYES. If they are cloudy, stay away. A fish's eyes should look like human eyes. Cloudy is bad. Period. It's not fish cataracts you're seeing, it's a fish that's been lying around on the ice too long.

2) LIFT THE GILLS and poke around under them. If it doesn't look rich and red, leave your green in your wallet. This is not the fish you want to serve your family and guests.

3) TOUCH THE FISH, POKE THE FISH. The flesh should bounce right back, and there should be no impression or indentation left.

4) IF IT SMELLS LIKE FISH, run for the hills.

Now, get started while the fish is still fresh!

[CONTINUED]

Crab Cakes with Avocado Salsa

4 TO 6 SERVINGS

FOR THE AVOCADO SALSA:

2 large ripe avocados, peeled, pitted,
    and coarsely smashed
1 small ripe tomato, diced
1/2 small red onion, finely diced
1/4 cup fresh corn, cooked
1/4 cup fresh peas, cooked
1/4 cup finely chopped fresh basil
Juice of 2 limes
2 tablespoons extra-virgin olive oil
Tabasco sauce
Salt

FOR THE CRAB CAKES:

1 medium zucchini, seeded, finely
    chopped, and squeezed dry
2 stalks celery, finely chopped
2 tablespoons capers, rinsed, finely
    chopped, and squeezed dry
1 large shallot, finely minced
1/2 cup ketchup
1/2 cup mayonnaise
Tabasco sauce
1 pound jumbo lump crabmeat,
    picked clean
1 cup packaged dried bread crumbs
1/2 cup sliced blanched almonds
1/2 cup extra-virgin olive oil

1. **TO MAKE THE AVOCADO SALSA:** In a large bowl, mix all the ingredients thoroughly. Adjust the seasonings to taste. Set aside.

2. **TO MAKE THE CRAB CAKES:** In a large bowl, mix the zucchini, celery, capers, shallot, ketchup, mayonnaise, and Tabasco to taste to make a dressing. Reserve 1/4 cup to garnish the crab cakes before serving. Gently fold the crabmeat into the dressing. Using a 1/2 cup measure form the crabmeat mixture into 4 to 6 balls.

3. Mix the bread crumbs and almonds in a small bowl. Thoroughly coat the crab balls in the bread crumb mixture. Flatten the crab balls to look like hockey pucks.

4. Preheat the oven to 400°F. In a large sauté pan over medium heat, pan-sear the crab cakes in the oil until golden brown, about 3 minutes, turning once.

5. Place the crab cakes on a baking sheet and bake for 5 to 6 minutes, or until cooked through.

6. To serve, place a generous spoonful of avocado salsa on a plate. Place a crab cake on the avocado salsa. Top with a small spoonful of the reserved dressing. Serve with potato chips.

Steamed Maine Mussels and Manila Clams

❧

THIS DISH REQUIRES ONLY 7 TO 8 MINUTES TO COOK;
DO NOT START UNTIL YOU'RE READY TO SERVE
4 TO 6 SERVINGS

5 to 6 dozen Manila clams (or cockles or other small clams)

4 to 5 dozen Maine mussels (or other mussels)

1/2 cup extra-virgin olive oil

3 garlic cloves, thinly sliced

3 shallots, minced

Large pinch of saffron threads

1/4 teaspoon fennel seed

1 teaspoon fresh thyme leaves

1/2 cup white wine

3/4 cup clam juice

1 tablespoon roughly chopped fresh basil

1 bunch arugula, washed thoroughly and roots trimmed off

1/2 cup sliced cherry tomatoes

Salt and freshly ground black pepper

1. Wash and scrub the shells of the clams and mussels with a vegetable brush. Remove the beards from the mussels and refrigerate until you are ready to assemble the dish. Discard any clams that are open, that do not close, or that do not smell fresh.

2. In a 14-inch stainless steel sauté pan with lid, heat the oil over high heat until it is lightly smoking. Lower the heat to medium low and add the garlic, shallots, saffron, fennel, and thyme. Sweat the vegetables, but do not brown them, about 2 minutes. Add the mussels and clams to the sauté pan and toss the mixture with a spoon. Deglaze with the wine and let it cook for 1 minute, then add the clam juice and cover with the lid. Do not reduce the heat. Allow the mussels and clams to cook for 3 minutes, or until they open.

3. Add the basil, arugula, and cherry tomatoes and season with salt and pepper to taste. Cover the pan and cook 1 minute, or until heated through. Serve warm.

NOTE: *A great accompaniment to this dish is crusty ciabatta bread rubbed with garlic, brushed with olive oil, and grilled. It is great for mopping up the wonderful broth from the clams and mussels.*

Grilled Salmon with White Bean, Sun-Dried Tomato, and Spinach Salad

6 SERVINGS

FOR THE SALMON MARINADE:

1/3 cup extra-virgin olive oil
Salt and freshly ground black pepper
Juice of 1 lemon
Juice of 1 orange
2 tablespoons chopped fresh basil
Six 8-ounce, 1-inch-thick boneless,
    skinless salmon fillets

FOR THE BALSAMIC VINAIGRETTE:

1/2 cup balsamic vinegar
1 teaspoon Dijon mustard
2 cups extra-virgin olive oil
Salt and freshly ground black pepper
2 minced shallots
3 tablespoons chopped fresh parsley
3 tablespoons chopped fresh basil

FOR THE SALAD:

2 pounds baby spinach, cleaned
2 cups cooked cannellini beans
1 roasted red bell pepper, cut into thin
    strips
1 roasted yellow bell pepper, cut into thin
    strips
1/2 cups thinly sliced sun-dried tomato

1. **TO MAKE THE MARINADE AND SALMON:** In a small bowl, combine the olive oil, salt and pepper to taste, lemon and orange juices, and basil.

2. Season the salmon with salt and pepper to taste. Brush the salmon with the marinade 1 to 2 hours before grilling, cover it in plastic, and refrigerate it. Pat the salmon dry before grilling to avoid flare up.

3. Lightly oil the hot grill and grill the salmon over very high heat, 3 to 4 minutes per side, until it is browned but the inside medium rare.

4. **TO MAKE THE BALSAMIC VINAIGRETTE:** In a medium bowl, combine the balsamic vinegar and mustard. Gradually whisk in the oil, then stir in salt and pepper to taste, the shallots, and fresh herbs.

5. **TO MAKE THE SALAD:** In a large bowl, toss the spinach with the beans, peppers, and sun-dried tomato. Dress the salad with the desired amount of vinaigrette. The balsamic vinaigrette can also be served as an accompanying sauce for the grilled salmon.

6. Place the salmon, hot off the grill, on top of the salad and serve.

Grilled Sea Scallops and Mushroom Skewers Wrapped with Pancetta, Lemon, and Fresh Herbs

❧

4 SERVINGS

2 pounds small to medium fresh sea
    scallops
1/3 cup extra-virgin olive oil
Juice and grated zest of 4 lemons
Cracked black pepper
1 tablespoon chopped fresh thyme
1 tablespoon chopped fresh oregano
2 tablespoons chopped fresh basil
2 tablespoons chopped fresh tarragon
About 20 fresh shiitake mushroom caps,
    stemmed
16 thin slices pancetta or bacon, cut
    into 2-inch pieces

1. Using your fingers, pull off and discard the small muscle from the side of any scallop that has one. Cut the medium sea scallops in half so that all the scallop pieces are the same size. Rinse the scallops under cold water, then blot them dry with paper towels. Set the scallops aside while you prepare the marinade.

2. In a medium bowl, combine the oil, lemon juice and zest, pepper to taste, and all of the herbs. Add the scallops and mushroom caps and toss to coat. Cover the bowl and marinate for 30 minutes.

3. Wrap each scallop with a piece of pancetta. Thread the scallops onto the skewers, placing a mushroom cap in between every other scallop.

4. Preheat the grill to high when you are ready to cook. Arrange the kebabs on the hot grill and cook until the scallops are firm and white, 1 to 2 minutes per side. Brush the scallops once or twice with remaining marinade before you take them off the grill.

5. Using a pair of tongs to hold the skewers at one end, use a fork to push the scallops off the skewers onto a serving platter.

Spiced Yellowfin Tuna with Chickpea
and Escarole Ragu

✻

6 SERVINGS

FOR THE SPICE RUB AND TUNA:

1 teaspoon ground coriander
1 teaspoon salt
1 teaspoon Chinese five-spice powder
1 teaspoon freshly ground black pepper
1 teaspoon ground fennel seed
1 teaspoon paprika or chili powder
2 pounds center-cut #1 sushi-grade
   yellowfin tuna
2 tablespoons extra-virgin olive oil

**FOR THE CHICKPEA AND
ESCAROLE RAGU:**

1/4 cup extra-virgin olive oil
2 red onions, thinly sliced
2 heads fennel, thinly sliced
2 heads escarole, washed, dried
   thoroughly, and ribbon-cut
One 14-once can beef broth
1 pound chickpeas, cooked according to
   package directions, or two 14-ounce
   cans chickpeas, rinsed under cold
   water

1. **TO MAKE THE SPICE RUB AND TUNA:** Combine the dry rub ingredients. Sprinkle the spices on both sides of the tuna. For heavier spice flavor, apply twice before searing the tuna. Preheat a heavy cast-iron skillet on high heat for 6 to 7 minutes.

2. Drizzle the olive oil in the skillet and add the tuna. Sear and lightly char evenly on both sides for a rare center. If you prefer the tuna cooked to greater doneness, remove the tuna from the skillet and cook in the oven at 350°F until cooked through, 5 to 10 minutes.

3. **TO MAKE THE CHICKPEA AND ESCAROLE RAGU:** Heat the olive oil in a large sauté pan over medium-low heat. Slowly cook the onion and fennel until nicely browned or caramelized, about 10 minutes. Add the escarole and cook 20 minutes, or until the escarole is fully cooked. Add the broth and chickpeas and simmer until heated through, about 5 minutes.

4. Serve the ragu on a large platter. Slice the tuna and arrange it on top of the ragu.

Basil-Studded Grilled Salmon Steak with Summer Salsa Cruda and Fresh Grilled Corn on the Cob

~

6 TO 8 SERVINGS

FOR THE CORN ON THE COB:

6 to 8 ears corn

FOR THE SALMON FILLETS:

Six to eight 6- to 8-ounce skinned and
 boned salmon fillets
24 to 32 fresh basil leaves
Sea salt and cracked black pepper
2 tablespoons extra-virgin olive oil
2 tablespoons fresh lemon and lime juice

FOR THE SALSA CRUDA:

3 large red tomatoes, peeled, seeded,
 and diced
3 large yellow tomatoes, peeled, seeded,
 and diced
1/2 pint mixed small cherry tomatoes,
 cut in half
4 cucumbers, peeled, seeded, and cut
 into small dice
2 garlic cloves, minced
1/2 small red onion, cut into small dice
1/2 cup extra-virgin olive oil
2 tablespoons red wine vinegar
Sea salt and cracked black pepper
1 tablespoon fresh thyme leaves
10 fresh basil leaves, thinly sliced
1 tablespoon chopped fresh oregano
1/3 cup chopped fresh flat-leaf parsley

1. **TO MAKE THE CORN ON THE COB:** Follow directions on page 145.

2. **TO MAKE THE SALMON FILLETS:** Place the salmon fillets on the cutting board, and with a small paring knife on a slight angle, make four ¾-inch-deep incisions in each.

3. Roll each basil leaf up like a tiny scroll and insert one into each incision until all the salmon fillets are studded with basil. You can make more than 4 incisions if desired.

4. When the studded salmon is complete and ready to cook, preheat the grill to high heat. Season the salmon with salt and pepper to taste and lightly brush the salmon with the olive oil and lemon and lime juice.

5. Arrange the salmon fillets on the hot grate and grill 3 minutes per side for medium doneness.

6. **TO MAKE THE SALSA CRUDA:** In a nonreactive bowl, combine the tomatoes, cucumbers, garlic, onion, oil, vinegar, and salt and pepper to taste. Toss gently to mix. This sauce should be highly seasoned. Just before serving the fish, gently mix in all the fresh herbs. (This preserves the herbs' flavor and color in the presence of the vinegar and tomato acids.) Spoon the salsa cruda on top of each fillet to serve.

Grilled Lobster and Summer Sweet Corn

✦

6 SERVINGS

6 ears sweet corn
1/3 cup extra-virgin olive oil
Salt
3/4 cup coarse sea salt
Six 1 1/2-pound lobsters
1 cup unsalted butter, melted, or
    extra-virgin olive oil

1. Turn the grill to medium 10 minutes before you're ready to grill. The corn will take 5 to 8 minutes longer than the lobsters, so start the corn before proceeding with the lobsters. Peel back the husks, keeping them attached to use as handles for grilling, and clean the silk from the kernels. Brush the corn with very small amount of olive oil. Season lightly with salt and begin grilling while preparing the lobsters. Grill the corn for 3 to 4 minutes, turning frequently.

2. In a large pot, bring 10 to 12 quarts of water with coarse salt to a rapid boil. The water should be very salty. One by one, plunge the lobsters into the boiling water for 1 minute, then remove.

3. Place the lobsters on the grill and cook for 8 to 10 minutes, turning frequently. The lobster will turn orange when it is done; you can also stick a fork into the tail meat to see if it comes out easily. To serve the lobsters, cut them in half lengthwise through the center of the head and tail and remove the gravelly stomach sac. Place the lobsters and corn on a large serving platter. Brush the lobsters and corn with melted butter or extra-virgin olive oil. Serve additional butter and olive oil in small dishes.

Pistachio-Crusted Sea Bass with Salsa Verde and Roasted Artichokes

6 SERVINGS

FOR THE ROASTED ARTICHOKES:

12 baby artichokes, washed
1/2 cup olive oil
Salt and freshly ground black pepper

FOR THE SEA BASS:

Six 8-ounce sea bass fillets
Salt and freshly ground black pepper
2 tablespoons whole-grain pommery mustard
1 cup finely chopped pistachios

FOR THE SALSA VERDE (MAKES 1 CUP):

1 cup finely chopped fresh basil
1 cup finely chopped fresh flat-leaf parsley
2 garlic cloves, crushed
2 ounces salted capers, well rinsed and finely chopped
3 anchovy fillets in oil, drained, rinsed, dried, and finely chopped
1 tablespoon red wine vinegar
2 1/2 tablespoons extra-virgin olive oil
2 teaspoons Dijon mustard
Salt and freshly ground black pepper

1. **TO MAKE THE ARTICHOKES:** Preheat the oven to 400°F. Cut the artichokes in half and toss with the olive oil and salt and pepper to taste. Place the artichokes on a baking tray and roast for 30 to 40 minutes, or until golden and tender.

2. **TO MAKE THE SEA BASS:** Reduce the oven temperature to 350°F. Season the fish with salt and black pepper to taste. Brush one side of each fillet with the mustard, then lightly coat that side with pistachios. Lay the fillets on a baking sheet, coated side up, and bake for 6 to 7 minutes, or until golden brown.

3. **TO MAKE THE SALSA VERDE:** In a medium bowl, place the herbs, garlic, capers, and anchovies. Whisking well, drizzle in the vinegar, then the oil. Flavor with the mustard, and salt and pepper to taste.

4. Place 4 artichoke halves in the center of each plate, top with a fillet of sea bass, and garnish with the salsa verde.

Grilled Salmon Cured with Dried Chamomile and Fresh Herbs with Rosemary Tuscan Fries

6 SERVINGS

FOR THE SALMON:

2 cups cold brewed chamomile tea
1/2 cup chopped fresh tarragon
1 cup salt
1/4 cup sugar
1/4 cup whole peppercorns
Six 8-ounce salmon fillets

FOR THE TUSCAN FRIES:

2 quarts frying oil
2 pounds potatoes, peeled and cut into
  1/2-inch matchsticks
6 fresh rosemary sprigs
Salt and freshly ground black pepper

1. **TO MAKE THE SALMON:** In a small mixing bowl, combine the chamomile tea, tarragon, salt, sugar, and peppercorns.

2. Place the salmon fillets on a tray with sides and pour the curing mixture on top. Cover in plastic wrap and cure in the refrigerator for about 24 hours.

3. Preheat the grill to high. Remove the fillets from the refrigerator and pat dry. Cook on the grill for about 8 minutes or until browned on the outside and medium-rare on the inside.

4. **TO MAKE THE TUSCAN FRIES:** In a deep-frying pot, heat the oil to 325°F. When the oil is hot, blanch the potatoes in the oil until they are golden brown, 4 to 5 minutes. Lay the potatoes on paper towels to rest until you are ready to serve them, then fry them again for 4 to 5 minutes. Frying them twice will make them crisper. If you desire, you can fry them once for 7 to 10 minutes, or until they are golden brown.

5. Just before serving, top the fries with the rosemary and salt and pepper to taste.

6. Place the salmon on a serving platter and serve with the fries.

Grilled Whole Branzino

～✦～

4 TO 6 SERVINGS

2 garlic cloves, crushed and roughly
    chopped
4 to 5 tablespoons extra-virgin olive oil
1 tablespoon roughly chopped fresh thyme
1 tablespoon roughly chopped fresh
    rosemary
Salt and cracked black pepper
Two 2 1/2- to 3 1/2-pound branzino (wild sea
    bass) or red snapper, gutted and scaled

1. In a small bowl, combine the garlic, olive oil, herbs, and salt and pepper to taste.

2. Brush the marinade over the branzino, inside and out. This can be done the day before you serve, or at least 2 to 3 hours before grilling. Refrigerate the fish, covered, until ready to grill.

3. If you're using a gas or electric grill, preheat the grill to high 10 to 15 minutes before cooking. If you're using wood or charcoal, start the fire 45 minutes to 1 hour ahead of time. Leave the cover off the grill the whole time.

4. Wipe off any marinade to keep the fire from flaring up. If you're using a grilling basket, place the basket over the heat source.

5. Grill the fish for a total of about 10 minutes per inch of thickness. Once the first side has nice dark grill marks, turn the fish carefully all at once to see if the fish is done. Insert a paring knife carefully into the back of the fish and gently pull the flesh away from the backbone. The flesh should pull away and appear moist. Transfer the fish to an oval platter and serve.

Pan-Roasted Wild King Salmon with Wild Fall Mushrooms, Roasted Butternut Squash, and Fingerling Potatoes

※

6 SERVINGS

FOR THE VEGETABLE GARNISH:

3 tablespoons olive oil
1 pound fingerling potatoes or small new potatoes, cut into 1/2-inch rounds
1 medium butternut squash, peeled, seeded, and cut into 1/2-inch cubes
5 to 6 ounces assorted wild mushrooms (preferably chanterelle, hen of the woods, porcini, or black trumpet*) trimmed, washed, dried, and sliced or cut into quarters
Salt and freshly ground black pepper

FOR THE SALMON:

Six 6-ounce portions wild king salmon, skin on, scaled, and pin bones removed
Salt and freshly ground black pepper
2 tablespoons olive oil
Aged balsamic vinegar

1. **TO MAKE THE VEGETABLE GARNISH:** In a medium sauté pan, heat the olive oil over medium heat. Add the potatoes and cook 8 to 10 minutes, or until lightly browned, and set aside. Add the butternut squash to the same pan and cook until the squash is lightly browned and soft, about 10 minutes. Add the mushrooms, stirring, and cook 5 minutes, or until golden brown. Season with salt and pepper to taste and set aside.

2. **TO MAKE THE SALMON:** Season the salmon with salt and pepper to taste on both sides. Heat the olive oil in a 12-inch nonstick sauté pan over medium to high heat. Cook the salmon for about 3 minutes per side, or until lightly browned. When the salmon is nicely browned on both sides, the fish should be done to medium and have an opaque center.

3. Arrange the pan-roasted vegetables on a large serving platter and top with the salmon. Spoon any remaining juices from the vegetables over the fish and vegetables and drizzling with balsamic vinegar. Serve immediately.

*Note: Cremini, oyster, or shiitake mushrooms may be substituted as well.

Pan-Seared Sea Scallops with Farro, Pumpkin, Swiss Chard, and Barolo Wine Sauce

⟨⟩

6 SERVINGS

½ pound pumpkin or butternut squash, seeded and peeled
Salt and freshly ground black pepper
7 tablespoons extra-virgin olive oil
3 tablespoons honey
2 tablespoons fresh lemon juice
½ small onion, minced
1 stalk celery, cut into small dice
1 garlic clove, crushed and minced
½ teaspoon fresh thyme leaves
2 cups farro or pearl barley
1 cup Barolo or other full-bodied dry red wine
2 quarts chicken broth or water
2 cups Swiss chard, ribs removed and cut into ½-inch ribbons, or fresh destemmed spinach
24 to 30 large sea scallops

1. Preheat the oven to 350°F. Cut the pumpkin into uniform 2-inch pieces. Season with salt and pepper to taste, drizzle with 2 tablespoons of the olive oil, and wrap in foil. Bake for 30 to 40 minutes, or until very soft. Remove the foil and place the pumpkin in a food processor. Add the honey and lemon juice and puree until smooth. Set aside.

2. In a heavy saucepan over high heat, add 3 tablespoons of the olive oil and sauté the onion, celery, garlic, and thyme until they are soft and light golden in color, about 3 minutes. Add the farro and sauté for 1 minute. Add the wine and cook down for 3 minutes. Add the broth and bring to a boil. Lower the heat to a simmer and cook until the farro is tender but still has a slight bite, about 20 minutes. Stir in the Swiss chard and pumpkin puree. Continue to cook, stirring, until all the liquid is absorbed into the farro, about 10 minutes. The farro should have the consistency of risotto and should not be soupy.

3. Season the scallops on both sides with salt and pepper to taste. In a heavy large nonstick pan on very high heat, add the remaining 2 tablespoons olive oil. In 3 small batches, quickly sear the scallops on both sides until they are just cooked but still moist.

4. Place the farro mixture on plates and top with the scallops.

Grilled Marinated Shrimp with Balsamic Glaze, Arugula, Cherry Tomatoes, Zucchini, and Summer Squash

❧

6 SERVINGS

FOR THE SHRIMP:

2 garlic cloves, minced
1 tablespoon lemon juice
1 teaspoon dried oregano
1/3 cup extra-virgin olive oil
Salt and freshly ground black pepper
1 tablespoon chopped fresh rosemary
1 tablespoon chopped fresh thyme
3 pounds large shrimp (about 48) peeled and deveined, tails intact
1 cup balsamic vinegar

FOR THE VEGETABLES:

4 zucchini
4 yellow squash
1 1/2 pounds arugula
1 quart multicolored sweet cherry tomatoes (any variety)
1/2 red onion, cut into small dice
1 garlic clove, finely minced
Salt and freshly ground black pepper
Olive oil

1. **TO MAKE THE SHRIMP:** In a large bowl, combine the garlic, lemon juice, oregano, olive oil, salt and pepper to taste, and fresh herbs. Place the shrimp in the bowl and toss with the marinade. Marinate in the refrigerator for 3 to 6 hours, covered.

2. Place the balsamic vinegar in a nonreactive saucepan and bring to a simmer over medium-low heat. Turn the heat to low and reduce to less than ¼ cup of glaze, 20 to 30 minutes. The glaze should be thick enough to coat the back of a spoon, but not sticky and thick.

3. Set the grill to high. Slice the zucchini and yellow squash lengthwise into ¼-inch-thick-strips. Grill for 2 minutes on each side or until browned. Remove from grill and cut into ½-inch bias strips. Put in a bowl with the arugula, tomatoes, onion, garlic, and salt and pepper to taste. Dress the vegetables with olive oil.

4. Set the grill to its highest setting. Remove the shrimp from the marinade, let drain for 2 minutes (do not pat dry), and grill for a total of 2 minutes, or until they turn pink, turning quickly so they cook evenly. Just before removing the shrimp from the grill, brush them with the balsamic glaze. Serve any extra balsamic glaze on the side.

Salmon Cartoccio

⦿

1 garlic clove, chopped
4 tablespoons olive oil
2 leeks, julienned
1 fennel bulb, julienned
1 carrot, julienned
2 tablespoons white wine
Salt and freshly ground black pepper
1 sprig fresh thyme
Two 6-ounce salmon fillets
¼ cup julienned fresh basil
2 egg whites
2 tablespoons flour

1. Preheat the oven to 375°F. In a large sauté pan over medium-high heat, sauté the garlic in 2 tablespoons of the olive oil. Add the leeks, then the fennel and carrot. Sauté about 5 minutes, or until the leeks are just translucent. Deglaze with the white wine, add salt and pepper to taste, and thyme. Do not overcook; the carrots should still be crunchy.

2. Place the vegetables on a 12-inch-square piece of parchment paper and top with the salmon. Add the basil, salt and pepper to taste, and top with the remaining 2 tablespoons olive oil.

3. In a small bowl, combine the egg whites and flour to make a paste. Brush the edges of the parchment paper with the paste.

4. Place a second square of parchment paper on top and fold the edges to form a tight seal.

5. Bake for 20 minutes, or until the parchment puffs up.

6. To serve, open the parchment, place the salmon and vegetable on plates, and drizzle the cooking juices on top.

Zuppa di Pesce

6 SERVINGS

4 tablespoons olive oil
1 carrot, finely diced
1 red onion, finely diced
1 stalk celery, finely diced
2 leeks, cleaned and finely diced
1 fennel bulb, finely diced
One 16-ounce can whole San Marzano
    tomatoes, with juice
1 teaspoon red pepper flakes
1 teaspoon dried oregano
2 cups dry white wine
One 16-ounce can clam juice
Salt
2 tablespoons chopped garlic
One 1-pound fillet sea bass, cut into
    4 pieces
12 large shrimp, peeled and deveined
20 Manila clams (or other small clams
    or cockles)
1 pound calamari, cleaned and cut into
    slices
12 mussels, cleaned
1 cup cooked cannellini beans (canned
    or fresh)
4 red tomatoes, diced
4 yellow tomatoes, diced
2 tablespoons chopped fresh basil

1. In a large sauté pan over medium heat, heat 2 tablespoons of the olive oil. Sauté the carrot, onion, celery, leeks, and fennel for 5 minutes. Add the canned tomatoes and cook for 10 minutes. Add the red pepper and oregano.

2. To deglaze the pan, add the wine and stir over medium heat for 10 minutes. Add the clam juice and cook over medium-low heat for 15 to 25 minutes, or until the flavors are melded and the sauce thickens slightly. Add salt to taste.

3. In a large sauté pan over low heat, sauté the garlic in the remaining 2 tablespoons olive oil for 2 to 4 minutes, or until golden brown. Pan-sear the fish for about 5 minutes total, turning once, until golden brown on each side. Set the sea bass aside on a plate. Add the shrimp to the pan and sauté 1 minute. Add the clams and calamari and sauté 1 minute (the clam shells will not open yet). Add the mussels and sauté 1 minute. Add the reserved sea bass and the sauce and cook 5 to 10 minutes over low heat, or until the clams and mussels open and the soup is the desired consistency. Add extra clam juice if the soup seems too thick.

4. Warm the cannellini beans over low heat. Drain them before serving.

5. Garnish with the diced tomatoes, cannellini beans, and chopped basil. Discard any unopened shellfish.

Baked Salmon Wrapped in Zucchini

6 SERVINGS

6 long zucchini
12 whole fresh basil leaves
1/2 cup chopped fresh parsley
1/2 cup grated Parmesan
Six 6- to 7-ounce skinned and boned
  salmon fillets
6 tablespoons extra-virgin olive oil
Salt and freshly ground black pepper
6 lemon wedges

1. Preheat the oven to 450°F. Slice each zucchini lengthwise into four ⅛-inch strips, discarding the sides. On a baking sheet, lay 2 of the zucchini strips next to each other and lay 2 more across them, to make a cross. Repeat with the remaining strips to make 6 crosses.

2. Place 2 basil leaves inside each zucchini cross. Sprinkle the fresh parsley and about ½ teaspoon grated Parmesan over the zucchini.

3. Place 1 salmon fillet in the center of each cross, then fold the zucchini strips over the fillet so that they overlap evenly. Turn the zucchini package over to hold the strips in place. Repeat with the remaining zucchini and salmon.

4. Drizzle about 4 tablespoons olive oil in a large casserole or nonstick baking pan. Place the zucchini-wrapped fillets in the pan with the overlapping side down and spaced at least an inch away from one another.

5. Brush the olive oil on top of the zucchini squares, season with salt and pepper to taste, and bake for 20 minutes, or until the zucchini strips are golden brown. Serve immediately with a drizzle of olive oil and a wedge of lemon.

Ahh, good old red meat. It's been in and out of diet favor for the last twenty years. Well, it's been in and out of favor everywhere except in the Scotto households, where it's as much a part of Sunday as the pasta, or as the grandparents used to say, "the macaroni." Seriously, how can you call it Sunday if there isn't any sausage, spinelli or pork chops, meatballs, or braciole simmering in the sauce—you remember, those "gravy meats" we talked about earlier in the book? We say if there are no gravy meats at a Sunday dinner, you may as well call it Friday!

Sure, over the past few years we've certainly accommodated guests who've given up meat, and we still do. But more and more we've seen our friends who've sworn off red meat forever swear back onto it when they go on high-protein diets.

All our dinner parties then, now, and always have included at least one kind of meat. In fact, we have a favorite butcher at whose feet we worship, and we've been known to pack coolers with his cuts before we drive out the country on weekends to ensure that we'll be serving the best beef and pork available.

When it's a grilling kind of Sunday, we even put an Italian spin on the good old American hamburger by smothering it in Gorgonzola cheese (yes, there's that cheese again!) and topping it off with pancetta. We also like serving grilled T-bone steaks with grilled red onions and sweet and hot chiles—a sure crowd pleaser.

Remember, when cooking the Sunday sauce, the gravy meats are usually served *after* the pasta. Leftover gravy meats are usually not only leftover but left *out*, or brought out again after dinner so that hungry hands can pick, pick, pick.

[CONTINUED]

Stewed Chicken with Tomatoes and Mushrooms

One 3-pound chicken
1/2 cup all-purpose flour
Salt and freshly ground black pepper
3/4 cup olive oil
1 tablespoon chopped garlic
1 cup chopped onion
1 cup halved button mushrooms
1/4 cup red wine vinegar
2 cups tomato sauce (see page 100)
1 cup chicken stock
1/2 bunch fresh basil, finely chopped

1. Cut the chicken into 8 pieces, leaving the bones in and the skin on.

2. Place the flour on a plate and season it with salt and pepper to taste. Lightly dust the chicken pieces with the flour.

3. In a large sauté pan over medium heat, heat ¼ cup of the olive oil and pan-sear the chicken on all sides until golden brown, about 4 minutes. Set aside the chicken.

4. In the same pan, heat the remaining ½ cup olive oil and sauté the garlic and onion until light brown, about 2 minutes. Add the mushrooms and sauté for 5 minutes, or until lightly browned. Deglaze with the red wine vinegar. Add the tomato sauce and stock and simmer over low heat for 5 minutes.

5. Add the chicken and cook on low heat for about 1 hour, or until the chicken is tender. Stir in the basil and season with salt and pepper to taste.

Herbed Roast Turkey

❧

One 12- to 14-pound turkey
1/4 cup olive oil
3 onions, sliced
5 carrots, peeled and cut in quarters
1 stalk celery, halved crosswise
1/2 cup fresh rosemary sprigs
1/2 cup fresh sage leaves
2 sticks unsalted butter
Kosher salt

1. Preheat the oven to 325°F. Remove the giblets and neck from the turkey and reserve for another use if desired. Rinse the turkey with cold water and pat dry. Coat a large roasting pan with the olive oil and stir in the onions, carrots, and celery.

2. Loosen the skin from the turkey breast a bit without totally detaching it. Place the rosemary and sage under the skin along with 1 stick of the butter, cut into small pieces. Smooth the skin over the herbs and put back into place.

3. Place the turkey breast-side up in the roasting pan (no rack is needed). Salt the turkey to taste and top with the remaining stick of butter, cut into pieces.

4. Roast the turkey until the meat thermometer (inserted deep into the turkey, but not touching the bone) registers about 180°F. This should take 3½ to 4 hours, but begin checking after 3 hours. Remove the turkey and let stand 15 minutes before carving.

Bollito Misto con Salsa Verde
(Mixed Boiled Meat with Green Sauce)

༺༻

FOR THE GREEN SAUCE:

Leaves from 5 bunches fresh flat-leaf
  parsley
7 canned anchovy fillets, drained
2 garlic cloves
1 to 2 tablespoons pickled capers, drained
2 teaspoons white wine vinegar
5 tablespoons olive oil
Salt and freshly ground black pepper

FOR THE BOILED MEAT:

2 onions, roughly chopped
4 carrots, roughly chopped
4 stalks celery, roughly chopped
2 small leeks, roughly chopped
2 pounds beef brisket or chuck steak
Salt and freshly ground black pepper
1 pound garlic-flavored pork sausage
1 pound veal (preferably sirloin tip)
One 3-pound chicken, cut in quarters
1 tablespoon minced fresh parsley

1. **TO MAKE THE GREEN SAUCE:** In a food processor, process the parsley leaves, anchovies, garlic, capers, and white wine vinegar until you get a smooth puree.

2. Gradually add the oil in a very thin stream until you get a smooth sauce. Season with salt and pepper to taste.

3. **TO MAKE THE BOILED MEAT:** In a Dutch oven or other large pot, combine the onions, carrots, celery, and leeks and add enough water to cover the vegetables by 3 to 4 inches. You may need as much as a gallon. Bring to a boil over high heat. Add the brisket and salt and pepper to taste, cover, and boil for 30 minutes. Add the sausage, veal, and chicken, reduce the heat, and simmer covered, for 1½ hours, skimming off the foam that rises to the surface.

4. Slice all the meats, including the sausage, and divide the chicken into suitable portions, placing everything on a large preheated platter. Before serving, make sure the meats are hot.

5. Add 1 cup of the meat broth to the platter of sliced meats. Sprinkle with fresh parsley.

6. Serve with the green sauce and boiled vegetables.

NOTE: *As a side dish, you may also serve steamed potatoes.*

NOTE: *Along with the green sauce, you may also want to use an additional dipping sauce,
such as the red pepper puree on page 168.*

Grilled Chicken Breasts with Red Pepper Puree and Grilled Asparagus

6 SERVINGS

FOR THE MARINADE:

3/4 cup extra-virgin olive oil
1/4 cup fresh lemon juice
4 tablespoons chopped fresh thyme
4 tablespoons chopped fresh parsley
4 garlic cloves, minced
2 shallots, minced
1/2 teaspoon salt
1/2 teaspoon freshly ground black pepper
1 pound fresh asparagus, tough ends trimmed
Six 6-to 8-ounce boneless chicken breasts

FOR THE RED PEPPER PUREE:

2 cups red bell peppers, thinly sliced
1/2 cup thinly sliced onion or shallots
2 garlic cloves, peeled and crushed
2 tablespoons extra-virgin olive oil
1 cup chicken stock
1 teaspoon balsamic vinegar
Salt and freshly ground black pepper

1. **TO MAKE THE MARINADE:** In a bowl, combine the olive oil, lemon juice, thyme, parsley, garlic, shallots, salt, and pepper. In separate containers, marinate the asparagus for about 10 minutes and the chicken for at least 1 hour in the refrigerator before grilling.

2. Heat the grill to high heat. Grill the chicken for 7 minutes per side, or until cooked through. Grill the asparagus for 4 minutes, turning once, or until lightly browned.

3. **TO MAKE THE ROASTED RED PEPPER PUREE:** Meanwhile, in a large sauté pan over medium heat, sauté the peppers, onion, and garlic in the olive oil until heated through.

4. Cover the pan and cook until the vegetables are soft, about 5 minutes.

5. Add the stock and simmer until the sauce is reduced and there is no free liquid visible on the bottom of the pan, 8 to 10 minutes.

6. Puree the vegetables in a blender until completely smooth. Stir in the balsamic vinegar and salt and pepper to taste. Adjust the consistency as needed; to thin the sauce, add a little water or stock.

7. Drizzle the sauce over the chicken and asparagus to serve.

Herb-Crusted Baby Rack of Lamb

⁊⁊

4 SERVINGS

¹/₂ pound fresh bread crumbs
¹/₄ cup mixed, finely chopped herbs
    (parsley, sage, rosemary, and thyme)
2 tablespoons chopped garlic
¹/₂ cup extra-virgin olive oil
4-pound whole rack of baby lamb
¹/₄ cup Dijon mustard

1. Preheat the oven to 450°F. In a bowl, combine the bread crumbs and chopped herbs. Add the garlic and oil and blend thoroughly.

2. Heat a large sauté pan over high heat and sear the rack of lamb, turning until dark brown on all sides, about 4 minutes. Allow it to cool for a minute. Brush the lamb with the mustard and roll the lamb in the bread crumbs to cover.

3. Place the rack of lamb in a roasting pan and roast for about 12 minutes, or until medium rare.

Prosciutto-Wrapped Pork Chops

⁊⁊

6 SERVINGS

6 bone in, center-cut pork chops (about
    10 ounces each, 4 pounds total)
1 tablespoon roughly chopped fresh rose-
    mary leaves
1 tablespoon roughly chopped fresh sage
    leaves
¹/₄ tablespoon freshly crushed black
    pepper
¹/₄ pound thinly sliced Parma prosciutto
¹/₄ cup extra-virgin olive oil

1. Preheat oven to 375°F. Season each side of the pork chops evenly with rosemary, sage, and pepper.

2. Wrap 2 pieces of the prosciutto in one continuous band around each pork chop until the prosciutto meets. Heat the olive oil in a 10-inch, preferably nonstick sauté pan over medium-high heat and brown the pork chops evenly on both sides, about 2 minutes per side.

3. Place the pork chops on a baking sheet and roast for 15 to 20 minutes for medium and 30 minutes for well done.

NOTE: *Center-cut pork chops should be at least 1 ½ inches thick and with the fat trimmed away from the bone.*

Grilled Sirloin alla Rollatina

∽

10 TO 12 SERVINGS

FOR THE SALSA CRUDA:

1 medium red onion, peeled and quartered
6 garlic cloves, peeled
1 jalapeño pepper, halved and seeded
6 to 8 fresh plum tomatoes, halved
4 tablespoons extra-virgin olive oil
2 tablespoons fresh lime juice
2 tablespoons balsamic vinegar
1/2 teaspoon dried oregano
1/4 cup chopped fresh flat-leaf parsley
1/4 cup chopped fresh basil
Salt and freshly ground black pepper

FOR THE STEAK ROLLATINA:

5 to 7 pounds trimmed sirloin or flank
   steak, butterflied*
3 roasted bell peppers, peeled and
   seeded**
4 garlic cloves, crushed with a knife blade
Salt and freshly ground black pepper
1 pound sliced provolone cheese
1 1/2 cups whole fresh basil leaves

1. **TO MAKE THE SALSA CRUDA:** Preheat the grill to high. Thread the onion quarters, garlic, and jalapeño peppers on skewers. Lightly brush the skewers and the tomatoes with olive oil and grill until the vegetables are lightly charred on all sides, 3 to 5 minutes.

2. Remove the vegetables to a plate and let cool. Remove the skewers.

3. Finely chop the onions, garlic, and jalapeño. Roughly chop the tomatoes, keeping them chunky. Place the vegetables and tomatoes in a large bowl. Add the remaining salsa ingredients, mix, and season with salt and pepper to taste.

4. **TO MAKE THE STEAK ROLLATINA:** Lay the butterflied steak on a cutting board with the longer end closest to you. Rub the beef with the garlic. Season the steak with salt and pepper to taste.

5. Overlap the slices of provolone on the beef until it is completely covered, like a sheet. Lay the basil leaves 2 inches apart on top of the provolone in order to cover evenly. Lay on the roasted bell peppers in the same way.

6. Roll up the steak and tie with butcher's twine at 1½-inch intervals. Season the outside of the meat with salt and pepper to taste.

7. Cut the meat crosswise in between the knot ties without cutting the twine. You should have nice 1½-inch pinwheels of beef rollatina. With a metal skewer, skewer the pinwheels through the beef to hold it together while grilling. Remove the twine.

8. Grill the rollatina about 3 minutes per side, or less if you want the beef rare. The cheese will melt and will brown like the beef.

9. Remove the rollatina from the grill and serve with the salsa cruda.

*NOTE: *If you use flank steak, ask the butcher to butterfly the steak and pound it lightly. Keep in the refrigerator until you are ready to use.*

**NOTE: *If you use canned or jarred peppers, fire-roasted are preferred. Lightly rinse and dry the peppers before using.*

Italian Grilled Burger

&⌘⌘

6 TO 8 SERVINGS

2 ¾ pounds ground round, chuck, or sirloin
1 tablespoon chopped fresh flat-leaf
  parsley
1 small garlic clove, crushed and finely
  chopped
Dash Worcestershire sauce
Dash Tabasco sauce
1 pinch dried Greek oregano
Salt and freshly ground black pepper
Olive oil
2 cups mild Gorgonzola cheese, cut into
  ½-inch-thick slices or crumbled, or
  mild blue cheese
6 to 8 ciabatta or other bread rolls
12 slices cooked pancetta* or bacon

1. In a medium bowl, mix together the meat, parsley, garlic, Worcestershire sauce, Tabasco sauce, and oregano. Season with salt and pepper to taste. Form patties 4 to 5 inches across and 1 inch thick.

2. Preheat the grill to its highest setting. Brush, clean, and rub the grill grate with an oiled towel before starting; this will allow a good sear and prevent the meat from sticking.

3. Brush the burgers with a tiny bit of olive oil and place them on the hottest part of the grill. Grill until the burgers are nicely browned, about 4 minutes per side for medium doneness.

4. After the burgers are almost done on the second side, top them with the Gorgonzola cheese. Also at this time, split the bread and place on the grill to be toasted. Place the grill cover down and cook the burgers until the cheese is melted. Keep an eye on the buns so they do not burn; they should only take about 30 seconds.

5. Remove the buns, place them on a platter, add a burger to each bun, and top with crispy pancetta.

NOTE: *What makes a great hamburger? The most important thing is the meat quality. You want to purchase a flavorful cut, like sirloin, chuck, or round. Ask the butcher to grind the meat at least twice, and it shouldn't be too lean; 20 percent fat is ideal. It's tempting to add more seasoning than the recipe calls for, but remember, less is more. You still want to taste the burger meat, so season lightly; your garnishes will give all the extra flavor you need. When handling the meat, make as few pats with your hands to form the patty as possible. Trying to make them perfectly round and smooth just robs them of flavor and texture. Lightly wet your hands with cold water before forming the patties to keep the meat from sticking to them.*

*NOTE: *Pancetta, an Italian bacon, is cured with salt and spices but not smoked; it's flavorful and slightly salty. It comes in a sausage-like roll; ask your butcher to slice it for you a little thicker than normal bacon slices, then cook them crispy as you would any bacon.*

Baked Pumpkin Stuffed with Sausage, Rice, and Mozzarella

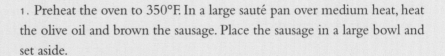

½ cup olive oil
1 pound Italian sausage without casing
1 onion, chopped (about 1 cup)
1 pound ground beef
1 pound ground veal
2 pounds uncooked rice
1½ pounds mozzarella cheese, diced
½ cup grated Parmesan cheese
1 medium pumpkin, top opened and
    seeds removed

1. Preheat the oven to 350°F. In a large sauté pan over medium heat, heat the olive oil and brown the sausage. Place the sausage in a large bowl and set aside.

2. In the same pan, sauté the onion, beef, and veal until brown, about 10 minutes, and add to the sausage.

3. Cook the rice as directed on the package. Mix the rice into the meat mixture. Stir in the mozzarella and Parmesan.

4. Mound the filling into the pumpkin and bake for about 20 minutes, or until the pumpkin is tender (stick a fork into it from the inside) and the mozzarella is melted. If not all the stuffing fits into the pumpkin, bake it on the side in a casserole.

5. To serve, scoop out the filling with a large spoon, capturing some of the pumpkin flesh as well.

Steak Pizzaiola with Sun-Dried Tomato Polenta

FOR THE STEAK PIZZAIOLA:

4 tablespoons olive oil
2 1/2 pounds beef tenderloin
3 garlic cloves, chopped
1 pound mushrooms, sliced
One 32-ounce can plum tomatoes,
   chopped
1/4 cup chopped fresh parsley
1 teaspoon dried oregano
Salt and freshly ground black pepper

**FOR THE SUN-DRIED
TOMATO POLENTA:**

3 cups milk
1 cup water
1 cup instant white polenta
1/2 cup mascarpone
2 tablespoons chopped garlic
2 tablespoons chopped shallots
1/4 cup extra-virgin olive oil
6 ounces sun-dried tomatoes

1. **TO MAKE THE STEAK PIZZAIOLA:** In a sauté pan, add 2 tablespoons of the olive oil and pan-sear the beef tenderloin over medium heat for a total of 2 to 3 minutes, turning to brown it thoroughly. Remove from the sauté pan and set aside.

2. Add the remaining 2 tablespoons olive oil, the garlic, and mushrooms to the pan and sauté for 2 to 3 minutes, or until golden brown.

3. Add the tomatoes, parsley, oregano, and beef tenderloin to the sauté pan and simmer over low heat for about 20 minutes or until the beef is cooked to your liking. Season with salt and pepper to taste.

4. **TO MAKE THE SUN-DRIED TOMATO POLENTA:** Heat the milk and water in a large pot and bring to a boil over medium heat. While it is simmering, slowly add the polenta. Stir constantly for 6 to 7 minutes, or until the liquid has been absorbed.

5. Remove the pan from the heat and stir in the mascarpone. Set the polenta aside.

6. In a medium pan, sauté the garlic and shallots in olive oil over low to medium heat until golden brown.

7. Add the sun-dried tomatoes and cook for 3 to 5 minutes, or until soft. Set aside.

8. Puree half of the sun-dried tomato mixture in a blender. Chop the other half.

9. To finish, combine the polenta, chopped sun-dried tomatoes, and pureed sun-dried tomatoes. Serve the polenta on plates and top with the steak.

Braised Pork Shoulder with Tomato, Fennel, Onion, and Barolo Wine

6 SERVINGS

FOR THE PORK SHOULDER:

One 7-pound boneless pork shoulder
Salt and freshly ground black pepper
3 tablespoons extra-virgin olive oil
2 fennel bulbs, finely diced
1 large carrot, finely diced
2 medium yellow onions, finely diced
4 large ripe tomatoes, peeled, seeded,
    and diced, with the juice strained
    and reserved
5 garlic cloves, thinly sliced
4 fresh thyme sprigs, finely minced
4 fresh rosemary sprigs, finely minced
2 whole bay leaves
1/2 bottle Barolo, Merlot, or Cabernet wine
2 quarts beef broth

FOR THE GARLIC MASHED POTATOES:

1 cup chopped garlic
1 tablespoon extra-virgin olive oil
Salt and freshly ground black pepper
2 pounds Idaho potatoes, peeled and cut
    in quarters
7 tablespoons unsalted butter
1 1/2 cup heavy cream

1. **TO MAKE THE PORK SHOULDER:** Preheat the oven to 350°F. Season the roast with salt and pepper to taste. Heat a large overproof stewing pan or large sauce pot over medium–high heat and brown the roast for 12 minutes, turning to brown on all sides. Transfer the roast to a plate.

2. In the same sauce pot add the olive oil, fennel, carrot, and onions and cook for 10 to 15 minutes, or until the onions are lightly browned. Add the tomatoes with the juices, garlic, and herbs and sauté for 5 minutes, then add the wine. Simmer to reduce by half and then add the meat broth.

3. Place the pork roast in the liquid. Cover the pot and place it in the oven. Roast until the meat is fork-tender, about 2 hours, or stick the roast with a skewer. If the meat is done, there will be no resistance as you push the skewer through the meat.

4. **TO MAKE THE GARLIC MASHED POTATOES:** Meanwhile, place the garlic on a baking sheet. Sprinkle the olive oil over the garlic and season with salt and pepper to taste. Cover with aluminum foil. Roast the garlic for 1 hour, or until tender.

5. Let the garlic cool and grind it into a paste with a food processor.

6. Place the potatoes in a saucepan full of cold water and bring to a boil. Cook for about 20 minutes, or until cooked through. Drain and set aside.

7. In another saucepan, melt the butter over medium-low heat, then add the cream and heat until it comes to a boil. Mix in the potatoes and garlic and mash to the desired consistency. Season with salt to taste.

8. When meat is done, skim away any fat from the braising liquid that appears on the surface. Test the consistency of the sauce by placing a spoonful on a plate. If a thin liquid bleeds out, reduce it further. The sauce will be quite thick.

9. Slice the roast, place the slices on the roasted garlic mashed potatoes, and cover the meat with the reduced sauce.

Grilled Sirloin Bracioles Stuffed with Provolone, Parmesan, Parsley, and Garlic

❧

FOR THE CHILE, RED ONION, AND CAPER RELISH:

2 bottled vinegar cherry peppers, seeds and stems removed, finely minced
3 tablespoons roughly chopped capers
1/2 small red onion, minced
2 garlic cloves, minced
1/2 cup chopped fresh parsley
1/2 cup extra-virgin olive oil
2 tablespoons fresh lemon juice
1 tablespoon Worcestershire sauce
Sea salt and cracked black pepper

FOR THE SIRLOIN BRACIOLES:

4 pounds trimmed sirloin steaks cut into 4-ounce slices and pounded to 1/8-inch thickness
1/3 cup extra-virgin olive oil
1/2 cup chopped fresh flat-leaf parsley
6 garlic cloves, minced
1 1/2 cups grated Parmesan or Romano cheese
1 pound provolone cheese, thinly sliced
Sea salt and cracked black pepper

1. **TO MAKE THE CHILE, RED ONION, AND CAPER RELISH:** In a medium bowl, combine the peppers, capers, onion, garlic, and parsley with the olive oil, lemon juice, and Worcestershire sauce.

2. Season the relish with the salt and pepper to taste, and let the mixture macerate at room temperature for 2 hours before serving.

3. **TO MAKE THE SIRLOIN BRACIOLES:** Lay the cutlets on a cutting board, brush them with the olive oil and season with the parsley, garlic, and Parmesan to taste. Place 1 or 2 thin slices of provolone on each cutlet and roll into a tight braciole. Roll with the ending seams of meat face up against one another so that the bracioles do not unravel while cooking. Repeat this process until all are complete. Line up the bracioles in four rows of 4 to 6. Using two steel skewers per row, pierce all the way through the rolls, until you have skewered all of them. Sprinkle with the salt and pepper.

4. Set the grill on high. Arrange the skewers on the grill and cook 3 to 4 minutes per side for medium doneness, or until the cheese slightly melts.

5. Remove the bracioles from the skewers and spoon the relish over them to serve.

Braised Veal Cheeks over Creamy Cheese Pumpkin Polenta

with Root Vegetable Ragu

6 SERVINGS

FOR THE VEAL CHEEKS:

1/2 cup plus 4 tablespoons olive oil
18 veal cheeks or six 2-inch veal shanks
    (about 2 pounds total)*
1 onion, cut into large dice
1 carrot, cut into large dice
1 stalk celery, cut into large dice
4 garlic cloves, crushed
Few sprigs fresh rosemary
Few sprigs fresh thyme
Few sprigs fresh parsley
4 tablespoons tomato paste
2 cups red wine
3 quarts beef or veal stock

FOR THE PUMPKIN POLENTA:

3 3/4 cup milk
1/2 cup heavy cream
1 tablespoon butter
1/2 teaspoon fresh thyme leaves
2 garlic cloves, crushed and minced
1 tablespoon extra-virgin olive oil
1/2 cup pureed cheese pumpkin
1/2 yellow cornmeal
1/4 cup grated Parmesan cheese
Salt and freshly ground black pepper

1. **TO MAKE THE VEAL CHEEKS:** Preheat the oven to 325°F. Heat ½ cup of the olive oil in a frying pan over high heat and sear the veal for 1 minute on each side, making sure that they are well browned evenly on both sides. Transfer the veal to a large casserole dish.

2. In a stew pot over medium heat, cook the remaining 4 tablespoons of olive oil, the vegetables, garlic, and herbs until golden brown, about 6 minutes. Add the tomato paste to the pot and cook for 5 minutes.

3. Spoon the vegetables and tomato over the veal in the casserole dish. Remove all the grease with a spoon and deglaze the pot with the red wine, stirring to loosen any food particles from the pot. Add the stock and cook for 10 minutes, over high heat to reduce.

4. Pour the contents of the pot over the veal, cover the casserole dish, and roast for 1½ to 2 hours, or until the meat is tender and can be pierced easily with a knife or skewer. Set the meat aside to cool in the liquid for at least 2 hours.

5. Carefully remove the meat and the vegetables to a plate and strain the braising sauce. Place all the liquid in a heavy saucepan. Simmer, uncovered, until the liquid is reduced to a rich glossy sauce, about 25 minutes. Serve the liquid on the side.

6. **TO MAKE THE PUMPKIN POLENTA:** Place the milk, cream, butter, thyme, garlic, and olive oil in a large saucepan and bring the mixture almost to a boil over medium heat.

7. Stir in ½ cup of the pumpkin puree (reserve the rest for another use) and whisk in the cornmeal in a steady stream until it is blended with no lumps. Continue to cook over low heat for 20 to 25 minutes, stirring constantly until the polenta is smooth and soft.

8. Just before you are ready to serve the polenta, stir in the Parmesan cheese and season with salt and pepper to taste. If you need to reheat the polenta, heat a little extra milk in a saucepan and gradually whisk into the cool polenta. Heat through, then stir in the cheese.

9. Serve the polenta on plates, topped with the veal cheeks.

*NOTE: *The butcher should clean the veal cheeks by removing the tough silver skin and gristle on one side of the veal cheeks.*

Lamb Pot Roast with Creamy Polenta

¼ cup olive oil
5 pounds lamb stew meat, cut into 2-inch
  pieces
2 ½ cups diced carrots
1 ½ cups diced onion
2 ½ cups diced fennel
1 tablespoon dried thyme
1 tablespoon dried oregano
2 cups port wine
1 quart veal stock
Salt and freshly ground black pepper
Creamy Polenta with Mascarpone Cheese
  (see page 199)

1. **TO MAKE THE LAMB:** Preheat the oven to 350°F. In a braising pan over high heat, heat the olive oil and pan-sear the lamb in single-layer batches until it is dark brown on all sides, about 5 minutes.

2. Add the carrots, onion, fennel, and herbs and cook for 5 minutes.

3. Add the port wine and simmer over medium heat until it is reduced by half, 15 to 20 minutes. Add the veal stock and season with salt and pepper to taste.

4. Cover and simmer for 30 to 45 minutes, or until the lamb is tender.

5. Top the creamy polenta with the lamb pot roast.

Marinated and Grilled Sicilian Leg of Lamb Steaks

❧

SERVE THIS WITH MARINATED GRILLED TOMATOES AND PEPPERS
WITH OLIVES AND ANCHOVIES (PAGE 202).
6 TO 8 SERVINGS

1 cup extra-virgin olive oil, plus extra
    for drizzling
6 garlic cloves, crushed
1 tablespoon kosher or sea salt
1 tablespoon cracked black pepper
1/3 cup roughly chopped fresh rosemary
1 teaspoon dried Greek oregano
Juice of 3 lemons
Eight 14- to 16-ounce lamb steaks*
Lemon wedges

1. In a medium bowl, combine the olive oil, garlic, salt, pepper, rosemary, oregano, and lemon juice. Place the steaks on a platter and spoon the marinade evenly over both sides of the steaks. Cover and marinate overnight in the refrigerator. Remove the platter from the refrigerator 1 hour before grilling.

2. Preheat the grill to high. Arrange the steaks on the hot grill grates. Grill the steaks, turning them with tongs, until they are cooked to taste, 5 to 6 minutes per side for medium rare.

3. Remove the steaks from the grill and place them on a serving platter. Drizzle the steaks with olive oil and serve with lemon wedges.

*NOTE: *The best choice for this dish would be steaks cut from the leg of lamb. Have your butcher cut steaks 1½ inches thick. Otherwise, use chops from the shoulder loin or rib.*

Maple- and Bourbon-Glazed Roast Pork Loin Stuffed with Apples and Sun-Dried Cranberries

6 SERVINGS

FOR THE GLAZE:

1/2 cup pure maple syrup
2 tablespoons unsalted butter
1 tablespoon Dijon mustard
1 teaspoon dark brown sugar
1 tablespoon fresh lemon juice
Salt and freshly ground black pepper
1/4 cup bourbon whiskey

FOR THE STUFFING:

1/2 cup sun-dried cranberries
3 tablespoons butter
1/2 onion, finely diced
1/4 cup finely diced celery
1 cup Granny Smith apples, peeled, cored, and coarsely diced
1/2 pound well-seasoned ground Italian sausage
1 pound breakfast sausage meat, casings removed, crumbled
1 cup fresh bread crumbs
1/2 cup chopped fresh parsley
Salt and freshly ground black pepper
One 5- to 6-pound boneless pork loin roast, split lengthwise down the middle for stuffing

1. **TO MAKE THE GLAZE:** Mix all the ingredients except the bourbon in a nonreactive saucepan and bring to a slow simmer over low heat. Cook, stirring, until the ingredients lightly coat a spoon. Add bourbon to the desired flavor. Set aside.

2. **TO MAKE THE STUFFING:** Reconstitute the cranberries in 1 cup of boiling water for 30 minutes or until soft, then drain and set aside.

3. Melt the butter over medium heat in a 10-inch sauté pan. Add the onion and celery and cook until soft, about 5 minutes. Add the apples and cook until all the moisture has evaporated and the mixture starts to stick, then add the cranberries. Transfer this mixture to a large bowl and let cool. When cool, add both kinds of sausage, the bread crumbs, and parsley. Season with salt and pepper to taste.

4. Preheat the oven to 400°F with the roasting pan inside. Spread the stuffing on the pork and roll up the loin. Fasten it securely with skewers and tie with butcher twine.

5. Place the loin on the preheated roasting pan and roast for 30 minutes, then reduce the heat to 325°F and roast until the internal temperature reaches 150°F, about 30 to 45 minutes. Let the loin rest for 15 to 20 minutes, then reheat the bourbon glaze in a small pan over low heat. Remove the skewers and twine, then brush the loin with the glaze. Slice the loin in 1/4-inch slices, arrange on a platter, and glaze again just before serving.

Grilled T-Bone Steak with Grilled Red Onions, Red Beans, and Sweet and Hot Chiles

❧

6 SERVINGS

FOR THE BARBECUE SAUCE:

3 tablespoons vegetable oil
1 medium onion, minced
1 garlic clove, minced
1/4 green bell pepper, minced
1 cup water
1/2 cup ketchup
1/2 cup tomato sauce
3 tablespoons cider vinegar (or more to taste)
1 heaping tablespoon minced chipotle peppers in adobo sauce (or more for added heat)
3 tablespoons Worcestershire sauce
2 tablespoons lemon juice
2 tablespoons pineapple juice
1/2 teaspoon Liquid Smoke
2 tablespoons molasses
4 tablespoons dark brown sugar
2 tablespoons Dijon mustard
1 teaspoon black pepper
1 teaspoon Old Bay spice mix
Four 14-ounce cans pinto beans, drained (or 1/2 pound dry pigeon beans, cooked according to package directions)

FOR THE GRILLED STEAK:

4 large sweet red onions, peeled and cut in 1/4-inch slices
4 green bell peppers, split in half and seeded
4 red bell peppers, split in half and seeded
1/2 cup olive oil
Salt and freshly ground black pepper
1/4 cup minced fresh cilantro
Three 1 1/2-pound T-Bone steaks, cut 1 1/2 inches thick
4 hot chiles (or thin red chili peppers)
4 jalapeño peppers (or hot yellow banana peppers)

1. **TO MAKE THE BARBECUE SAUCE:** The night before your meal, heat the oil in a large nonreactive sauce pan over medium heat. Add the onion, garlic, and bell pepper. Sauté until soft, about 10 minutes.

2. Stir in the remaining sauce ingredients except the beans. Bring to a boil, stirring so that the mixture does not scorch. Reduce the heat to low and simmer, uncovered, until thickened, 15 to 25 minutes. If the sauce becomes too thick, add a little water. Remove from the heat and taste; the sauce should be highly seasoned. Adding cider vinegar and hot pepper is very necessary for the flavor of this sauce. Add the prepared beans and mix thoroughly.

3. **TO MAKE THE GRILLED STEAK:** Start a charcoal fire or turn the grill to its highest setting. In a large bowl, toss the onions and red and green peppers with the olive oil, and salt and pepper to taste. Grill until nicely charred and soft, about 5 minutes. Set aside and sprinkle with the cilantro.

4. Season the steaks heavily with salt and pepper to taste and grill to desired doneness, about 8 minutes per side. Let rest for 5 minutes before serving. Throw the chiles and jalapeños on the grill for a few seconds to warm them.

5. Top each steak with the grilled peppers and onions and the chiles and jalapeños. Serve the hot beans and barbecue sauce on the side.

Braised Short Ribs with Roasted Garlic Mashed Potatoes

⌘

1/2 cup olive oil

6 pounds beef short ribs, cut 2 inches
   wide

Salt and freshly ground black pepper

1 cup diced prosciutto

1 1/2 cups finely grated carrots

2 cups finely grated onion

1 cup finely grated fennel (1 trimmed bulb)

1/4 cup chopped garlic

1 tablespoon grated lemon zest

1 tablespoon grated orange zest

1 1/2 cups tomato puree

1 cup red wine

1 cup beef stock

1 1/2 teaspoons crushed red pepper flakes

Garlic-Roasted Mashed Potatoes
   (page 177)

1. Preheat the oven to 375°F. In a large, heavy skillet, heat the oil over medium-high heat. Season the short ribs with salt and pepper to taste, and put about a third of them into the skillet. Sear until browned, 2 to 3 minutes per side. Transfer the seared ribs to a large roasting pan. Sear the remaining ribs in batches, taking care not to crowd the pan.

2. Reduce the heat to low, add the prosciutto to the same skillet, and cook for 10 to 12 minutes, until the fat is rendered. Carefully pour off the fat and discard, keeping the prosciutto in the skillet.

3. Add the carrots, onion, fennel, and garlic and cook, covered, for about 20 minutes, or until the vegetables soften. Add the lemon and orange zest, tomato puree, wine, stock, and red pepper flakes. Season to taste with salt if necessary and cook for about 5 minutes longer.

4. Pour the sauce over the ribs in the roasting pan. If necessary, add more stock or water so that the liquid comes three-quarters of the way up the sides of the ribs. Cover tightly with aluminum foil and roast for 1½ hours. Remove the foil and roast for about 1 hour longer, or until the ribs are very tender.

5. Transfer the ribs to a warm serving platter. Pour the remaining sauce into a saucepan, bring to a boil over medium-high heat, and cook until it is reduced to about 3 cups. Pour the sauce over the ribs to serve.

6. Serve with the potatoes.

Marinated and Grilled Flank Steak

✦

4 TO 6 SERVINGS

2 tablespoons minced garlic
2 tablespoons minced shallots
¼ cup chopped fresh thyme
¼ cup chopped fresh oregano
1 cup extra-virgin olive oil
6 tablespoons balsamic vinegar
2 ½ pounds flank steak
Salt and freshly ground black pepper

1. Combine the garlic, shallots, thyme, oregano, olive oil, and balsamic vinegar in a bowl and mix well. Brush the flank steak with the marinade and marinate, covered, overnight in the refrigerator.

2. Preheat the grill to high. Sprinkle the steak with the salt and pepper to taste. Place the flank steak on the hot grill and cook 7 to 10 minutes, turning once, until desired doneness.

NOTE: *Flank steak should be cut on a bias against the grain.*

Italian Dry-Rub BBQ Ribs

✦

6 TO 8 SERVINGS

FOR THE DRY RUB:

2 tablespoons ground fennel seed
3 tablespoons sweet paprika
2 tablespoons brown sugar
1 tablespoon granulated sugar
1 tablespoon cayenne pepper
1 tablespoon dried rosemary
1 tablespoon dried thyme
1 tablespoon dried oregano
3 tablespoons minced fresh garlic
1 tablespoon salt

FOR THE RIBS:

Six 1 ¾-pound slabs pork baby back
    spareribs
½ cup extra-virgin olive oil
Juice of 4 lemons
Juice of 2 oranges

1. TO MAKE THE DRY RUB: In a medium bowl, mix the dry rub ingredients with your hands.

2. TO MAKE THE RIBS: The night before serving the ribs, sprinkle half of the dry rub ingredients on both sides of the ribs. Tightly cover the ribs and refrigerate overnight.

3. Mix the other half of the dry rub mix with the olive oil and citrus juices and set aside for basting.

4. Preheat the grill to its lowest setting. Cook the ribs slowly, basting and turning them every 30 minutes, for 1½ hours, or until the bones can easily be pulled from the meat. Turn the grill to medium if the ribs are not cooking fast enough.

*J*ust when you think that Sunday dinner *must* be complete by now, along come the side dishes. We like to think that side dishes are like side*cars*: they aren't driving the dinner, but they're not just along for the ride either. Just as sidecars are used to carry extra people and goods, side dishes are used to carry the extra bits of flavor that may be missing from your meal. But make no mistake, side dishes also enhance the meal and complement the entrées.

So what the heck's the difference between a "side" and a veggie? A side may *contain* mostly vegetables (and usually does), but they are vegetables with *more*, like stuffing, for example. Of course, Scotto sides, like all things Scotto, are probably a bit different from what you might be used to. Because our sides are on the side doesn't mean they're on a fast-food menu. In fact, chances are good that unless you're ordering out tonight from Tuscany (which might take awhile—hope you're not too hungry), you're not going to find, say, Zucchini Blossoms with Ricotta, Pecorino, and Mozzarella. It may sound exotic, but to us, it's still a side dish.

Our personal favorite side dish? Easy: it's Mom's rice stuffing for turkey, which isn't just rice of course—it's mixed with mushrooms, sausage, onions, and gooey mozzarella! The "stuffing" isn't actually *stuffed* into the turkey, but cooked separately. It's so delicious that we usually make two to three times the amount we'll need because we eat it as a meal the next day. In other words, the side becomes the front!

Most of the other sides you'll find here are on the lighter side—except of course, when we melt (here it is again!) Gorgonzola over the fingerling potatoes. We can't help it. We're Gorgonzola junkies. Maybe the Scotto family needs to enroll in a Gorgonzola twelve-step program! But that's just an, er, aside.

Sides

Sicilian Potato Salad

2 1/2 pounds small Yukon gold potatoes or
    small red bliss potatoes
1 cup extra-virgin olive oil
6 tablespoons red wine vinegar
2 tablespoons balsamic vinegar
3/4 cup chopped fresh flat-leaf parsley
4 tablespoons chopped capers
1/2 cup chopped pitted mixed olives
1 tablespoon chopped anchovies
1 tablespoon minced garlic
1 tablespoon salt
1/4 teaspoon red pepper flakes
2 tablespoons chopped fresh oregano or
    1 tablespoon dried oregano

1. In a large pot, simmer the unpeeled potatoes in lightly salted water over medium heat until they are just cooked through.

2. In a medium bowl, mix the olive oil, red wine vinegar, balsamic vinegar, parsley, capers, olives, anchovies, garlic, salt, pepper flakes, and oregano.

3. Drain the potatoes and let them air dry in a strainer to remove any excess moisture. Leave the potatoes unpeeled. Cut the potatoes in half and place in a large bowl.

4. Pour the dressing over the potatoes. Let it rest at room temperature for at least 30 minutes so the flavors have a chance to be absorbed by the potatoes. Serve at room temperature or refrigerate until you are ready to serve.

Sautéed Spinach

4 tablespoons extra-virgin olive oil
3 garlic cloves, thinly sliced
1 bunch spinach, washed and dried
    (3 pounds)
1 teaspoon red pepper flakes
Salt and freshly ground black pepper

1. Place the olive oil in a heavy saucepan over medium heat. Add the garlic and sauté for 5 minutes, or until lightly browned.

2. Remove the garlic from the pan and set aside. Add the spinach and sauté until it is soft but still bright green and firm, about 2 minutes. Add in the garlic and pepper flakes and sauté for 2 to 5 minutes more, or until the spinach is the desired texture. Season with salt and pepper to taste.

Sautéed Broccoli Rabe

❧

2 TO 4 SERVINGS

4 tablespoons extra-virgin olive oil
3 garlic cloves, thinly sliced
2 bunches broccoli rabe, tender tops
  and tender stems only, cut into
  3- to 4-inch pieces
1 teaspoon red pepper flakes
Salt and freshly ground black pepper

1. Place the olive oil in a heavy saucepan over medium heat. Add the garlic and sauté for 5 minutes, or until lightly browned.

2. Remove the garlic from the pan and set aside. Add the broccoli rabe and sauté until it is soft but still green and firm, about 2 minutes. Add in the garlic and pepper flakes and sauté 5 to 10 minutes more, or until the broccoli rabe is the desired texture. Season with salt and pepper to taste.

Grilled Asparagus

❧

2 TO 4 SERVINGS

1 bunch fresh green asparagus, peeled
    and trimmed* (about 1 pound)
1 tablespoon extra-virgin olive oil
Salt and freshly ground black pepper

Preheat the grill to high, lightly brush the asparagus with the olive oil, and season with salt and pepper to taste. Grill the asparagus just until tender, about 2 minutes per side. Serve immediately.

*NOTE: *If asparagus are pencil size, there is no need to peel, just trim 2 inches off the base. If the asparagus are large, they need to be peeled.*

Creamy Polenta with Mascarpone Cheese

❧

6 SERVINGS

3 cups milk
1 cup water
1 cup instant polenta
Salt and freshly ground black pepper
1/2 cup mascarpone cheese

1. Heat the milk and water in a large pot and bring to a boil. While it is simmering, slowly add the polenta and salt and pepper to taste. Stir constantly for 6 to 7 minutes, or until the liquid has been absorbed.

2. Remove from the heat and stir in the mascarpone.

Zucchini Blossoms Filled with Ricotta, Parmesan, Pecorino, and Mozzarella, Baked with Tomato Sauce

6 SERVINGS

2 cups fresh ricotta cheese
1 cup freshly grated Parmesan cheese
1/2 cup grated Pecorino Romano cheese
1 pound fresh mozzarella, cut into
    small dice
1/2 cup chopped fresh parsley
2 tablespoons extra-virgin olive oil, plus
    extra for drizzling
Salt and freshly ground black pepper
18 zucchini flowers (about 1 pound), rinsed
    very gently and set aside to dry*
2 cups tomato sauce

1. In a medium bowl, combine the ricotta, ½ cup of the Parmesan, the Pecorino Romano, mozzarella, parsley, and olive oil. Thoroughly season with salt and pepper and place in a pastry bag without a tip. If you do not have a pastry bag, you can use a small teaspoon to fill the zucchini flowers.

2. Taking each flower by the stem, carefully open the flower, insert the pastry bag, and gently squeeze the cheese filling into the flower. Be careful not to overfill the flower; leave enough room at the end to fold under the whole flower. Repeat until all the flowers are filled.

3. Choose a low casserole or baking pan that will hold the blossoms snugly. Spread the tomato sauce on the bottom of the casserole and place the flowers on top.

4. Preheat the broiler 10 minutes before serving.

5. Lightly drizzle the olive oil on top of the blossoms, sprinkle with the remaining ½ cup Parmesan cheese, and broil until light golden brown, 5 to 7 minutes.

*NOTE: *Zucchini blossoms are in season from about June to September.*

Marinated Grilled Tomatoes and Peppers

with Olives and Anchovies

❧

6 TO 8 SERVINGS

3 red bell peppers, stemmed, seeded, and
  cut in half

3 yellow bell peppers, stemmed, seeded,
  and cut in half

3 green bell peppers, stemmed, seeded,
  and cut in half

2 tablespoons olive oil

Kosher or sea salt and freshly cracked
  black pepper

6 tomatoes, any variety

1 teaspoon dried oregano

6 fresh basil leaves, thinly sliced

2 to 4 oil-packed anchovies, drained and
  cut into 1/4-inch pieces

2 tablespoons drained capers

2 tablespoons balsamic vinegar

1/2 cup cured Sicilian olive oil

1. Preheat the grill to high. In a medium bowl, toss the peppers with 1 tablespoon of the olive oil and salt and pepper to taste.

2. In another medium bowl, toss the tomatoes with the remaining 1 tablespoon olive oil, and salt and pepper to taste.

3. Arrange the peppers on the hot grate and grill, turning them with tongs, until they are blistered and nicely browned all over, about 5 minutes. Then begin grilling the tomatoes, which will take about half the time of the peppers. When the tomatoes are evenly grilled on the tops and bottoms and soft (about 2 minutes total), remove to a serving platter and arrange nicely.

4. Sprinkle the peppers and tomatoes with the oregano, basil, anchovies, and capers before serving; finish with a drizzle of balsamic vinegar and Sicilian olive oil.

Vegetable Kabobs with Zucchini, Peppers, Yellow Squash, and Eggplant

6 SERVINGS

2 tablespoons Dijon mustard
1/2 cup extra-virgin olive oil
1/4 cup balsamic vinegar
1 tablespoon chopped garlic
2 medium green zucchini
2 medium yellow squash
2 medium eggplant
3 red bell peppers
Salt and freshly ground black pepper

1. Combine mustard, oil, vinegar, and garlic in a medium bowl to make a marinade.

2. Cut the zucchini and squash into ½-inch-thick half-moons. Slice the eggplant into ½-inch-thick rounds and then cut into quarters. Cut each red pepper into 1-inch squares.

3. Place the vegetables in the marinade bowl, stir, and marinate for 30 minutes. Preheat the grill to medium high. Place the vegetables on skewers, alternating types.

4. Grill the kabobs for 2 to 3 minutes per side or until the vegetables are nicely browned.

Grilled Fingerling Potatoes with Gorgonzola Cheese

2 SERVINGS

1 pound medium to large fingerling
   potatoes, cut in half lengthwise
1/2 cup butter, at room temperature
1/2 cup crumbled Gorgonzola cheese
1/2 cup chopped fresh flat-leaf parsley
Kosher salt and freshly ground black
   pepper

1. Preheat the grill. Cook the potatoes in salted boiling water until they are cooked through but not soft, 7 to 9 minutes. Remove the potatoes from the water and immediately submerge them in ice water to stop the cooking. Remove the potatoes from the water and pat dry. Set aside.

2. In a small mixing bowl, combine the butter and ¾ of the Gorgonzola cheese. Mix well and set aside.

3. Place the potatoes flesh-side down over the hot coals and grill for 1 ½ to 2 minutes. Turn the potatoes over and grill for 1 more minute. In a large bowl, combine the potatoes, butter and cheese mixture, and parsley. Toss gently, being careful not to break the potatoes. Add salt and pepper to taste.

4. Place the potatoes on a serving plate for two to share and sprinkle with the remaining Gorgonzola cheese.

Sausage and Rice Turkey Stuffing

⚬⚬⚬

10 TO 15 SERVINGS

¼ cup extra-virgin olive oil
1 pound Italian sausage without casing
1 onion, chopped
1 pound ground beef
1 pound ground veal
2 pounds uncooked
1½ pounds mozzarella cheese, diced
½ cup grated Parmesan cheese

1. Preheat the oven to 350°F. In a large sauté pan over medium heat, brown the sausage in 1 tablespoon of the olive. Remove it to a large bowl. Sauté the onion, beef, and veal in the remaining 2 tablespoons olive oil until brown and add it to the bowl.

2. Cook the rice according to the package directions. In a large bowl, stir together the rice, mozzarella, and Parmesan.

3. Place the mixture in a casserole dish and bake for 20 minutes, or until the cheese is melted.

hew! Are you full yet? Oh, c'mon—there's always room for dessert. It's called the next notch on your belt. If you think that we Italians only treasure three desserts—biscotti, cannoli, and tiramisù—have we got a sugar shock in store for you.

Okay, so our favorite insanely yummy desserts may *not* be your everyday white-bread cupcakes. But this is not your everyday white-bread cookbook (or so we'd like to think!). This is the sinful Scotto Sunday cookbook— you know—from soup to Pistachio Mascarpone Tort, you might say.

Our Sunday cookbook wouldn't be complete without desserts any more than our Sunday dinners would be complete before the last cup of cappuccino has been served and the last guest exclaims, "Okay! That's it! I can't eat another bite!" So that means we've included a slew of homemade desserts that will have your guests begging to be invited back.

Since, as you may have noticed, we like to get the kids involved early and often (the family that bakes together stays together), we have even included plenty of desserts that are both kid-easy and grown-up delicious. Our brood of lots of little kids loves nothing more than helping Grandma Marion make the desserts on Sundays—although they inevitably fight over who gets the "lickers" (the beaters from the electric mixer) once they're done. What kid wouldn't want to assemble our Chocolate Oreo Ice Cream Pie—and what grown-up doesn't want to eat it? (You in the back row on the diet—sit down!)

We've even included a bunch of breads that are especially perfect for brunch, but that are so yummy that we consider them desserts, too. Such as? How about Lemon, Chocolate, and Maple Zucchini Breads, or a not-too-sweet toasted Panettone with Spiced Mascarpone and Orange Supremes?

And if you have a sweet tooth that just won't quit, we offer a Bittersweet Chocolate Pudding that might make you a hedonist and a Peach Upside Down Cake that's so good it could seduce the skinniest socialite into a bite or three.

So, sit down, eat something. You're too thin anyway!

No. . . . We're not just cannoli.

[CONTINUED]

Chocolate Zucchini Bread

❧

24 SERVINGS

3 cups all-purpose flour
1 teaspoon salt
1 teaspoon ground cinnamon
1/4 teaspoon baking powder
1 teaspoon baking soda
3 eggs
2 cups white sugar
1 cup vegetable oil
1 teaspoon vanilla extract
2 cups grated zucchini
Two 1-ounce squares unsweetened
    chocolate, melted and set aside to cool
1 cup chopped almonds

1. Preheat the oven to 350°F. Grease two 9 × 5-inch loaf pans.

2. In a medium bowl, sift together the flour, salt, cinnamon, baking powder, and baking soda.

3. In a large bowl, beat the eggs until they are lemon-colored. Beat in the sugar and oil. Stir in the vanilla, zucchini, and chocolate. Mix the dry ingredients into the zucchini mixture just until blended; do not overmix. Stir in the chopped almonds. Pour the batter into the prepared pans.

4. Bake for 1 hour, or until a tester inserted in the center comes out clean. Cool the bread in the pans for 15 to 20 minutes, then flip the bread onto the racks to finish cooling.

Maple Zucchini Bread

❧❧

24 SERVINGS

3 eggs
1 cup vegetable oil
1 cup packed brown sugar
1 cup white sugar
3 teaspoons maple-flavored extract
2 1/2 cups all-purpose flour
2 teaspoons baking soda
1/2 teaspoon baking powder
2 teaspoons salt
2 cups grated zucchini
1 cup chopped walnuts

1. Preheat the oven to 325°F. Grease two 9 × 5-inch bread pans.

2. In a large mixing bowl, beat the eggs. Add the oil, sugars, and maple extract, and mix until foamy.

3. Blend in the flour, baking soda, baking powder, and salt. Stir in the zucchini and walnuts. Pour the batter into the prepared pans.

4. Bake for 1 hour, or until a tester inserted in the center comes out clean. Cool before serving.

NOTE: *Maple-flavored extract is much more intensely flavored than maple syrup. It can be found in baking supply stores.*

Lemon Zucchini Bread

❧❧

12 SERVINGS

1 1/2 cups all-purpose flour
1 teaspoon ground ginger
1 1/2 teaspoons baking powder
1/4 teaspoon salt
1 cup sugar
1/4 cup vegetable oil
2 eggs, slightly beaten
2 tablespoons freshly squeezed
    lemon juice
1 tablespoon freshly grated lemon peel
1 cup shredded zucchini
1/2 cup chopped walnuts

1. Preheat the oven to 350°F. Grease and flour a 9 × 5 × 3-inch loaf pan.

2. In a large mixing bowl, stir together the flour, ginger, baking powder, salt, and sugar. Add the oil, eggs, lemon juice, lemon peel, shredded zucchini, and chopped walnuts. Stir to blend, but do not overmix.

3. Spoon the batter into the prepared loaf pan. Bake for 45 to 55 minutes, or until a wooden pick inserted into the center of the loaf comes out clean. Cool the zucchini bread in the pan on a wire rack for 5 to 10 minutes, then flip the bread onto the rack to finish cooling.

Bittersweet Chocolate Pudding Cake with Vanilla Gelato

✺

6 TO 10 SERVINGS

FOR THE PUDDING CAKE:

1 ³/₄ cups flour
¹/₄ teaspoon salt
1 teaspoon baking soda
¹/₂ cup plus 2 tablespoons unsweetened
    cocoa powder
1 cup butter
1 ³/₄ cups firmly packed light brown sugar
4 eggs
1 teaspoon vanilla extract
Store-bought vanilla gelato

FOR THE BUTTERSCOTCH SAUCE:

1 pound light brown sugar
¹/₂ pound butter
1 cup heavy cream
¹/₈ cup light corn syrup

1. **TO MAKE THE PUDDING CAKE:** Preheat the oven to 350°F. Sift together the flour, salt, baking soda, and ½ cup of the cocoa powder.

2. In a large bowl, beat the butter and 1 cup of the brown sugar at medium speed until light. Add the eggs, one at a time, beating well after each addition. Beat in the vanilla. Stir in the sifted dry ingredients.

3. Lightly grease a 2-quart baking dish. Spoon the batter into the dish.

4. In a small bowl, mix together the remaining ¾ cups light brown sugar, 2 tablespoons cocoa powder, and ¾ cup hot water. Pour this liquid over the batter and place the baking dish into a larger pan. Add enough hot water to the larger pan to reach halfway up the baking dish.

5. Bake 40 to 45 minutes, or until the pudding is barely set and has begun to pull away from the sides of the baking dish.

6. **TO MAKE THE BUTTERSCOTCH SAUCE:** Combine all the ingredients in a small saucepan, bring to a boil over medium heat, and remove from the heat. Serve the warm pudding with the butterscotch sauce and vanilla gelato on top.

Arborio Rice Pudding

1 quart plus 1 cup heavy cream
2 cups whole milk
3/4 cup Arborio rice
3 whole eggs
5 egg yolks
1 cup sugar
1 tablespoon vanilla extract
1 1/2 teaspoons ground cinnamon
2 teaspoons orange flower water
   (available in specialty food stores)
1 cup chopped dates

1. Preheat the oven to 350°F. In a medium saucepan, combine 1 quart of the heavy cream, the milk, and rice. Bring to a boil over high heat, stirring constantly. Cover and simmer over low heat for 20 minutes, or until creamy.

2. In a large bowl, whisk together the eggs, egg yolks, sugar, vanilla, cinnamon, and orange flower water. Set aside.

3. Add a small amount of the hot liquid into the egg mixture, mix well, and then add the rest. Stir in the remaining 1 cup cream and the chopped dates.

4. Pour the mixture into a 4-quart casserole dish. Place the dish in a larger pan and put the pan in the oven. Pour enough hot water into the larger pan to fill it halfway. Bake the pudding for 40 to 45 minutes, or until set.

NOTE: *It's important to track down the orange flower water—it really makes the dish.*

Lavender Pots de Crème

❧

6 SERVINGS

2 cups light cream (half and half)
3 tablespoons dried lavender flowers
    (available in natural food stores)
6 egg yolks
1/2 cup sugar
1/8 teaspoon salt
1/2 cup whipped cream
Candied violets (optional) (available in
    baking supply stores)

1. Preheat the oven to 350°F. Boil a large pot of water and set aside.

2. In a medium saucepan over medium heat, heat 1¾ cups of the light cream (half and half) and the lavender flowers until the cream is scalding, but not boiling. Remove the pan from the heat and set aside.

3. In a medium bowl, beat the egg yolks until they are lemon colored. Beat in the sugar, salt, and the remaining ¼ cup of the light cream.

4. Gradually beat the hot cream into the egg yolk mixture, stirring constantly.

5. Strain the mixture into a medium bowl.

6. Place 6 pots de crème cups (or small soufflé cups, custard cups, or 6-ounce ramekins) in a large roasting pan. Divide the mixture evenly into the 6 cups. Pour enough of the hot water in the pan to come halfway up the sides of the cups (this is called a water bath). Cover the pan with aluminum foil or with the pot lids. Bake until the custard is just set around the edges, about 30 to 35 minutes.

7. Carefully remove the pan from the oven. Leave the pots de crème in the water bath and allow the pots de crème to cool to room temperature. Remove the pots de crème from the water bath, cover them with plastic wrap, and chill in the refrigerator for at least 2 hours or up to overnight.

8. Serve the pots de crème garnished with a spoonful of whipped cream and candied violets.

NOTE: *The pots de crème may be chilled in the refrigerator for up to 2 days.*

Zucchini Cake

❧

12 SERVINGS

FOR THE CAKE:

1 cup vegetable oil
2 cups sugar
3 eggs
2 teaspoon pure vanilla extract
2 cups flour
1/2 teaspoon baking powder
2 teaspoons cinnamon
1 teaspoon baking soda
2 cups grated zucchini (leave the skin on)
1 cup chopped walnuts

FOR THE ICING:

1/2 cup melted butter
One 8-ounce package cream cheese
1 teaspoon vanilla
1 pound confectioner's sugar

1. **TO MAKE THE CAKE:** Preheat the oven to 350°F. Grease and flour two 9-inch cake pans. In a medium bowl, mix the oil and sugar. Add the eggs, one at a time, beating well after each addition. Blend in the vanilla.

2. In a separate bowl, sift together the flour, baking powder, cinnamon, and baking soda.

3. Stir the sifted dry ingredients into the egg mixture, then stir in the zucchini. Fold in the walnuts. The batter will be a bit thin.

4. Pour the batter into the prepared pans. Bake for 45 minutes, or until a cake tester inserted into the middle comes out clean. Let cool.

5. **TO MAKE THE ICING:** In a small bowl, combine the butter, cream cheese, and vanilla. Gradually add the confectioner's sugar. Beat until the icing is smooth.

6. Ice the cooled cake and serve.

Bittersweet Chocolate Pudding

❧

FOR THE PUDDING:

1 cup sugar
1/4 cup cornstarch
1/4 teaspoon salt
3 cups milk
3 egg yolks, slightly beaten
2 tablespoons butter
2 teaspoons vanilla extract
2 1/2 ounces unsweetened chocolate,
    finely chopped

FOR THE WHIPPED TOPPING:

1 container (500 grams) mascarpone
    cheese
2 cups heavy cream
1/4 cup sugar
1 teaspoon vanilla extract

1. In a medium saucepan, combine the sugar, cornstarch, and salt. Stir in the milk, blending well. Cook over medium heat, stirring constantly, until the mixture boils and thickens. Boil for 2 minutes. Remove the pan from the heat. Blend a small amount of the hot mixture into the egg yolks. Return the egg mixture to the saucepan, blending thoroughly. Cook over medium-low heat until the mixture just begins to bubble, stirring constantly. Remove the pan from the heat, stir in the butter, vanilla, and chocolate. Cover with plastic wrap to keep the skin from forming on the surface of the pudding and refrigerate.

2. After the pudding has set about 1 hour, whip together the topping ingredients in a large bowl. Whip until stiff, spread over the pudding, and return to the refrigerator for at least 2 more hours.

3. Serve chilled.

Chocolate Fondue

❧

6 ounces semisweet chocolate, chopped
1/3 cup heavy cream
2 tablespoons Grand Marnier, brandy,
    or rum (optional)
Assorted fruits, cut into bite-size pieces,
    or marshmallows

1. Gently melt the chocolate over hot water in a double boiler or heat in the microwave on medium power for 2 to 4 minutes; blend until smooth. Whisk in the cream. Stir in the liqueur, if desired. Transfer the mixture to a serving dish or fondue pot.

2. Serve warm with the fruit or marshmallows.

Apple and Pear Crisp with Almond Crumb Topping

6 SERVINGS

FOR THE ALMOND CRUMB TOPPING:

1 cup light brown sugar
1 cup granulated sugar
1/2 cup all-purpose flour
1 teaspoon cinnamon
1 cup cold butter
1 teaspoon vanilla extract
1 teaspoon almond extract
3 cups chopped almonds

FOR THE FRUIT FILLING:

6 medium apples, peeled, cored, and sliced
6 medium pears, peeled, cored, and sliced
1 cup sugar
3/4 cup all-purpose flour
1 tablespoon grated orange peel
1 tablespoon grated lemon peel

1. **TO MAKE THE ALMOND CRUMB TOPPING:** In a medium bowl, combine the sugars, flour, and cinnamon. Cut in the cold butter, but do not overmix. You want to make crumbs, not a dough.

2. Sprinkle the vanilla and almond extracts over the crumbs, then fold in the walnuts. Set aside.

3. **TO MAKE THE FRUIT FILLING:** Preheat the oven to 350°F. In a medium saucepan, combine the apples, pears, sugar, and flour, and cook over medium heat until the fruit just begins to soften. Stir in the orange and lemon peels.

4. Place the fruit in a 12 × 8-inch baking dish. Cover with the almond crumb topping.

5. Bake for 35 minutes, or until the fruit is tender and the topping is browned. Serve warm.

Chocolate Tortellini in Pear Broth

❧

4 SERVINGS

FOR THE POACHED PEARS:

4 well-shaped medium pears
3 cups white wine, preferably chardonnay
3/4 cup sugar
3 cups pear nectar
2 lemons, sliced
1 cinnamon stick
2 tablespoons Armagnac or other
   fine cognac

FOR THE GANACHE:

3 tablespoons heavy cream
1 tablespoon orange zest
3 ounces bittersweet chocolate, chopped
3 tablespoons unsalted butter

1. **TO MAKE THE POACHED PEARS:** Peel and core the pears. Slice them in half lengthwise and place in a shallow sauce pan. Pour the wine, sugar, and pear nectar over the pear halves. Add the lemons and cinnamon. Bring to a boil and reduce to a simmer. Cook just until the pears soften, about 10 minutes. Remove from the heat and let the pears cool in the liquid.*

2. **TO MAKE THE GANACHE:** Stir the cream, orange zest, chocolate, and butter in a double boiler over barely simmering water until melted. Strain through a fine mesh sieve and refrigerate, covered, for 2 hours, or until firm.

3. **TO MAKE THE PASTA:** Combine the cocoa and hot water in a small bowl and stir to make a paste. Place the cocoa mixture, melted chocolate, egg, semolina flour, and sugar in an electric mixer fitted with a dough hook and blend for 5 minutes, or until the ingredients are combined.

4. Remove the dough from the mixer and knead by hand until smooth, adding a little more flour if the dough is too sticky.

5. Cover the dough with plastic wrap and refrigerate for 1 hour. Roll the dough out on a floured surface to a 1/16-inch thick rectangle and cut it into twenty-four 2 1/2-inch squares.

FOR THE CHOCOLATE TORTELLINI:

1 tablespoon cocoa
1 tablespoon hot water
1 tablespoon melted bittersweet chocolate
1 egg, at room temperature
3/4 cup semolina flour
2 tablespoons sugar
1 egg, beaten

6. **TO MAKE THE TORTELLINI:** Place about 1 teaspoon of the ganache in the center of each square.

7. Brush 2 of the edges with the beaten egg, fold over the square to form a triangle, and pinch the edges to seal.

8. Pull the 2 points on the long side together and pinch firmly to form the tortellini.

9. Drop the tortellini into simmering water for 3 minutes, or until they float. Drain and set aside.[†]

10. **TO MAKE THE SOUP:** Drain the poaching liquid from pears into large saucepan. You will be starting with about 4 cups; reduce this to 3 cups over medium-high heat. At a full boil, this takes 10 to 15 minutes.

11. Add the tortellini[‡] and Armagnac to the reduced pear broth.

12. Heat the soup bowls. Fan cut (do not cut completely through the narrow end so that when slightly flattened, the pear slices fan attractively) and lay a pear half at the side of each bowl. Ladle in the broth and tortellini to serve.

*NOTE: *Poached pears should be made a day or more in advance to allow the flavor of the broth to develop.*

†NOTE: *The tortellini may be made a day in advance. Store it in a single layer covered in plastic in the refrigerator.*

‡NOTE: *The pasta must be cooked close to serving time; the dough will lose its texture if it remains in the broth for too long, especially if kept warm.*

Angel Food Cake with Strawberries in Grappa

ᏇᏇ

8 SERVINGS

FOR THE ANGEL FOOD CAKE:

2 cups plus 3 tablespoons all-purpose flour
2 1/4 cups granulated sugar
2 1/4 cups egg whites
1 1/2 teaspoons cream of tartar
Pinch of salt
1 tablespoon vanilla extract
3/4 teaspoon almond extract

FOR THE STRAWBERRIES:

4 cups sliced strawberries
1/2 cup sugar
1/4 cup grappa

1. **TO MAKE THE ANGEL FOOD CAKE:** Preheat the oven to 350°F. Sift together the flour and ¾ cup of the sugar twice and set aside.

2. In a medium bowl, combine the egg whites with the cream of tartar and salt. Whipping on high, slowly add the remaining 1½ cups sugar and continue beating until the egg whites form stiff peaks. Add the vanilla and almond extracts, then the flour/sugar mixture, combining thoroughly, but do not overmix. Pour the batter into a 10-inch ungreased 2-piece tube pan and bake for 40 minutes. Cool the cake upside down.

3. **TO MAKE THE STRAWBERRIES:** Combine the ingredients in a medium bowl and toss gently. Let the strawberries sit at room temperature for 30 minutes, tossing periodically.

4. Serve the strawberries over the angel food cake.

Pistachio Mascarpone Tort

12 SERVINGS

FOR THE PISTACHIO TORT:

6 large eggs, separated
1 ¼ cups sugar
¼ teaspoon salt
1 teaspoon vanilla
1 teaspoon pistachio extract
⅛ teaspoon cream of tartar
2 ¼ cups very finely chopped pistachios
2 tablespoons flour

FOR THE MASCARPONE CREAM:

6 tablespoons sugar
3 large egg yolks
3 tablespoons flour
¾ cup milk
1 ½ packages (12 ounces total) chilled
    mascarpone cheese

1. **FOR THE PISTACHIO TORT:** Preheat the oven to 350°F. Line the bottoms of two greased 9-inch round cake pans with parchment paper; grease the paper and flour the pans lightly.

2. Beat the egg yolks at high speed in a large bowl for 2 minutes. Gradually beat 1 cup of the sugar into the egg yolks, and continue beating until the eggs are very thick and lemon colored, about 3 to 5 minutes. Beat in the salt and vanilla.

3. Using clean beaters, beat the egg whites and cream of tartar in a large bowl until soft peaks form. Add the remaining ¼ cup sugar gradually, beating until stiff peaks form.

4. Toss the pistachios with the flour. Fold ½ of the egg whites into the egg yolk mixture. Then, fold in ½ of the pistachio-flour mixture. Repeat with the remaining egg yolk and pistachio mixtures. Spread the batter into the prepared pans.

5. Bake until the cakes are firm to the touch and are beginning to pull away from the sides of the pans, about 35 to 40 minutes. Cool the cakes in the pans, upside down, on wire racks until the pans are cool, about 15 to 20 minutes. Remove the cakes from the pans, loosening the sides of the cakes with a sharp knife if necessary. Remove the parchment paper and cool completely.

6. FOR THE MASCARPONE CREAM: In a small bowl, whisk the sugar into the egg yolks, then whisk in the flour. In a medium saucepan, heat the milk over medium heat to a boil. Gradually whisk ½ the milk into the yolk mixture; then whisk the yolk mixture into the saucepan with the remaining milk. Whisk over medium heat until the mixture boils and thickens, about 2 to 3 minutes. Pour into a medium bowl and cool. Cover and refrigerate until chilled.

7. Let the mascarpone cheese stand at room temperature in a medium bowl until it is soft enough to stir, 10 to 15 minutes. Whisk the chilled egg yolk mixture into the cheese until smooth.

8. To assemble, place 1 cake layer on a serving plate and spread with 1 cup of mascarpone cream. Top with the second cake layer and spread the top of the cake with the remaining mascarpone cream. Refrigerate the cake overnight; let it stand at room temperature for 15 to 30 minutes before serving.

Grilled Tropical Tart with Pineapple, Mango, and Banana

∞

FOR THE GRAHAM CRACKER CRUST:

1 ³/4 cups graham cracker crumbs
1/3 cup cake flour
1/4 cup granulated sugar
3/4 cup unsalted butter, melted

FOR THE TART FILLING:

1 (8-ounce) container mascarpone cheese
3/4 cup sugar
2 teaspoons rum extract
1 pineapple, cored and thinly sliced
3 mangos, peeled and thinly sliced
4 bananas, peeled

1. **TO MAKE THE GRAHAM CRACKER CRUST:** Preheat the oven to 350°F. In a large bowl, combine the graham cracker crumbs, cake flour, sugar, and butter. Press the mixture into the bottom and sides of a 9-inch pie pan. Bake the crust for 12 minutes. Set the crust aside.

2. **TO MAKE THE TART FILLING:** Preheat the grill. In a medium bowl, combine the mascarpone, ½ cup of the sugar, and rum extract. Spread the mixture evenly over the prepared graham cracker crust.

3. Sprinkle the fruit with the remaining ¼ cup of the sugar and grill just until the sugar caramelizes. Layer the grilled fruit on top of the mascarpone cream mixture. Refrigerate the tart for 1 hour before serving.

Spiced Pumpkin Fudge

∞

3 cups sugar
3/4 cup butter or margarine
One 5 ¹/3-ounce can (²/3 cup)
   evaporated milk
1/2 cup solid pack pumpkin
1 teaspoon pumpkin pie spice
One 12-ounce package butterscotch
   morsels
One 7-ounce jar marshmallow creme
1 cup chopped toasted almonds
   or pecans
1 teaspoon vanilla extract

1. Grease a 13 × 9-inch pan. In heavy saucepan, combine the sugar, butter, milk, pumpkin, and spice. Bring the mixture to a boil over medium heat, stirring constantly until the mixture reaches 225°F, about 10 minutes.

2. Remove the pan from the heat. Stir in the butterscotch morsels. Add the marshmallow creme, nuts, and vanilla. Mix until well blended.

3. Quickly pour the mixture into the prepared pan, spreading just until even. Cool at room temperature. Cut into squares. Store tightly wrapped in the refrigerator.

Panettone Bread Pudding

❧

6 SERVINGS

1 pound panettone (traditional Italian fruit cake), cut into 1/2-inch cubes
3 cups heavy cream
3 cups whole milk
8 large egg yolks
1 cup plus 3 tablespoons sugar
2 tablespoons finely chopped orange zest
1 teaspoon pure vanilla extract
1 tablespoon unsalted butter
8 ounces semisweet (dark) chocolate, coarsely chopped
Sweetened whipped cream, for garnish

1. Preheat the oven to 200°F.

2. Spread the panettone cubes in a single layer on a baking sheet and toast for 30 to 40 minutes, or until dried out.

3. In a large bowl, combine the cream, milk, egg yolks, 1 cup of the sugar, orange zest, and vanilla extract. Whisk gently until the sugar dissolves. Add the panettone to the bowl and set aside to soak for 30 minutes.

4. Increase the oven temperature to 350°F.

5. Rub the butter over the bottom and sides of a 2-quart glass or ceramic baking dish about 8 × 12 × 2 ½-inches deep. Sprinkle the remaining 3 tablespoons of sugar over the butter.

6. Stir the chocolate into the panettone mixture and then pour the mixture into the baking dish. Set the dish in a larger pan and add enough hot water to come halfway up the sides of the dish. Bake for 45 to 50 minutes, until the surface is golden brown and firm and the custard is set. Remove the dish from the water bath and set aside to cool for 20 minutes. Serve warm, garnished with whipped cream.

NOTE: *Panettone is a traditional Italian fruit cake sold in Italian markets and specialty stores. One small commercially available cake is about 16 ounces.*

Peach Upside Down Cake

❧

6 SERVINGS

1 ½ cups butter
¾ cup brown sugar
8 peaches, peeled, pitted, and sliced
2 cups sugar
4 eggs
4 cups all-purpose flour
2 teaspoons baking powder
2 teaspoons baking soda
1 teaspoon salt
2 cups sour cream
2 teaspoons almond extract

1. Preheat the oven to 325°F. Melt ½ cup of the butter in a 10-inch cake pan. Sprinkle the brown sugar evenly over the butter.

2. Arrange the peach slices over the butter-sugar coating.

3. In a medium bowl, cream the remaining 1 cup butter and the sugar until light and fluffy. Add the eggs, one at a time, mixing well. In a medium bowl, sift together the flour, baking powder, baking soda, and salt. Stir the flour mixture into the batter in batches, alternately with sour cream. Mix in the almond extract.

4. Pour the mixture on top of the peaches and bake for 45 minutes (or until a wooden pick stuck into the center of the cake comes out clean). Remove the cake from the oven and invert the cake pan onto a plate. Leave the pan there for a few minutes, so the butter-sugar can run out of the pan onto the cake.

5. Serve warm or at room temperature.

Pumpkin Ricotta Fritters

❧

25 TO 30 FRITTERS

1 cup whole milk ricotta
1 cup solid pack pumpkin
4 eggs
¹⁄₄ cup powdered sugar, plus more
    for garnish
¹⁄₂ cup all-purpose flour
¹⁄₂ cup cake flour
1 tablespoon baking powder
2 teaspoons ground cinnamon
2 teaspoons ground ginger
1 teaspoon ground nutmeg
1 pinch salt
1 quart vegetable oil for frying
Honey, for garnish

1. In a large bowl, combine the ricotta, pumpkin, eggs, powdered sugar, flours, baking powder, spices, and salt and mix until smooth.

2. Drop heaping tablespoons into hot (350°) oil and fry until golden brown.

3. Dust with powdered sugar and drizzle with honey to serve.

Orange Blossom Pound Cake

❧

12 SERVINGS

2 cups butter, softened
4 ¹⁄₄ cups sugar
4 ¹⁄₂ cups sifted cake flour
2 ¹⁄₄ teaspoons baking powder
¹⁄₂ teaspoon salt
¹⁄₂ cup milk
9 eggs
3 tablespoons orange flower water
    (available in specialty food stores)
Zest of 3 oranges, minced
2 cups orange juice

1. Preheat the oven to 350°F. Grease and flour a Bundt pan. In a large bowl, cream the butter together with 2 ¼ cups of the sugar. Add the flour, baking powder, and salt and mix until well combined. Add the milk, eggs, 1 tablespoon of the orange flower water, and orange zest and beat until smooth. Pour the batter into the Bundt pan.

2. Bake for 1 hour and 15 minutes, or until a toothpick inserted into the middle of the cake comes out clean. Poke holes all over the cake with a toothpick and let it cool thoroughly.

3. In a small saucepan, combine the orange juice, the remaining 2 cups of sugar, and the remaining 2 tablespoons of orange flower water. Bring to a boil over high heat. Paint the sauce onto the cake with a pastry brush.

Blueberry Strawberry Shortcake

❧

4 cups flour

1/4 cup sugar, plus extra for sprinkling and to sweeten the cream

3/4 teaspoon salt

1 cup unsalted butter (very cold)

1 cup vegetable shortening (very cold)

1/2 cup buttermilk

1 quart strawberries, hulled and sliced

1 quart blueberries

3 cups heavy cream, whipped

1. Preheat the oven to 325°F. In a large mixing bowl, mix together the flour, sugar, and salt. Cut in the butter and shortening until the mixture resembles coarse sand. Add the buttermilk and mix just until the dough comes together in a ball. Wrap in plastic and refrigerate for 2 to 3 hours. Roll the dough on a lightly floured surface and cut three 10-inch circles. Prick them with a fork, sprinkle liberally with sugar, and bake for 25 to 30 minutes.

2. TO CONSTRUCT: Place one pastry disk on a serving plate and top with 1/3 of the strawberries, blueberries, and whipped cream. Make three layers total with the remaining pastry, berries, and cream. Serve immediately.

Heart-Shaped Banana Caramel Napoleon

❧

6 TO 8 SERVINGS

Puff pastry sheets (available frozen at the grocery store)

2 cups prepackaged caramel sauce

1 container (500 grams) mascarpone cheese

4 bananas, sliced

1. Cut the pastry sheets into whatever shape you wish (hearts for Valentine's Day) and bake according to the package instructions.

2. Combine the caramel sauce and mascarpone cheese and whip until stiff peaks form.

3. Layer the pastry with the caramel cream and banana slices and serve.

Blood Orange Panna Cotta

❦

FOR THE CARAMEL:

1/2 teaspoon lemon juice
1/2 cup granulated sugar
2 tablespoons hot water

FOR THE CREAM:

2 cups freshly squeezed blood
    orange juice
2 envelopes unflavored gelatin
4 cups heavy cream
1 cup sugar

1. **TO MAKE THE CARAMEL:** Put the lemon juice and sugar in a heavy pot. Cook over high heat, swirling often, until the sugar caramelizes. Add the hot water carefully as the caramel will splatter. Pour the caramel into the bottom of a 2-quart mold or bowl.

2. **TO MAKE THE CREAM:** In a small saucepan, place the orange juice and sprinkle the gelatin over it. Set aside to soften.

3. In another saucepan, combine the cream and sugar, and heat just enough to dissolve the sugar.

4. Heat the orange juice and gelatin gently to melt the gelatin.

5. Combine the orange juice mixture and the cream mixture. Pour into the prepared mold and refrigerate overnight.

6. Invert the panna cotta onto a serving platter just before serving.

Chocolate Oreo Ice Cream Pie

✦

6 SERVINGS

FOR THE CRUST:

1 ½ cups finely crushed Oreo cookie
    crumbs (crush 15 cookies in a food
    processor or blender)
3 tablespoons butter, melted

FOR THE FILLING:

1 quart vanilla ice cream, softened
1 cup fudge sauce
1 cup coarsely chopped Oreo cookies

1. **TO MAKE THE CRUST:** Generously butter a 9-inch glass pie plate. In a large bowl, stir together the cookie crumbs and butter. Using your fingertips, firmly and evenly press the mixture into the bottom and sides of the pie pan.

2. **TO MAKE THE FILLING:** Spread ½ of the ice cream in the prepared crust. Top with the fudge sauce, then spread the rest of the ice cream on top of the sauce. Sprinkle with the chopped cookies. Freeze until the pie is firm.

3. Cut into wedges to serve.

Kiwi Lime Tart

❧

6 SERVINGS

One 14-ounce can sweetened
    condensed milk
4 egg yolks
1 cup freshly squeezed lime juice
1/2 teaspoon cream of tartar
One 9-inch graham cracker pie crust
10 to 12 peeled and sliced kiwis
1/4 cup water
1/2 cup sugar
1 tablespoon cornstarch
1/2 teaspoon grated lime zest

1. Preheat the oven to 350°F. In a medium bowl, combine the milk, egg yolks, 1/2 cup of the lime juice, and cream of tartar. Pour the mixture into the pie shell and bake for 8 to 10 minutes. Remove the pie from the oven and refrigerate until firm.

2. Arrange the kiwi slices over the top of the lime custard.

3. In a medium bowl, combine the water, the remaining 1/2 cup lime juice, sugar, cornstarch, and lime zest. Bring the mixture to a boil over high heat and cook until thickened. Brush the glaze over the fruit and serve.

Toasted Panettone with Spiced Mascarpone and Orange Supremes

❧

6 SERVINGS

1 panettone (traditional Italian fruit cake)
6 oranges
One 8-ounce container mascarpone
4 tablespoons honey
1 tablespoon dark rum
1 teaspoon ground ginger
1 teaspoon ground cinnamon
1 teaspoon grated orange peel
1/4 teaspoon ground nutmeg
1/4 teaspoon ground cloves

1. Preheat the oven to 350°F. Slice the panettone horizontally into 1-inch slices and toast for 7 to 9 minutes, or until nicely brown.

2. In a medium bowl, mix the mascarpone with the honey, rum, and spices.

3. Peel and segment the oranges, cutting away the white pith and membranes to leave just the fruit.

4. Cut the panettone in triangles and place 2 pieces in each bowl. Top with a scoop of the mascarpone mixture and spoon the oranges over the top.

Chestnut Cheesecake with Caramel Sauce

6 TO 10 SERVINGS

FOR THE GRAHAM CRACKER CRUST:

7 ounces graham cracker crumbs
1/4 cup cake flour
1/4 cup granulated sugar
3/4 cup unsalted butter, melted

FOR THE CHESTNUT FILLING:

1 cup canned chestnut purée
3/4 cup sugar
2 pounds whole milk ricotta
1 1/2 teaspoons vanilla extract

FOR THE CARAMEL SAUCE:

2 cups sugar
1/4 cup water
1/2 cup heavy cream

1. TO MAKE THE GRAHAM CRACKER CRUST: Preheat the oven to 350°F. In a medium bowl, combine all the ingredients and mix well. Press the mixture onto the bottom of a 10-inch springform pan that has been covered with aluminum foil. Bake for 12 minutes and set aside.

2. TO MAKE THE CHESTNUT FILLING: Reduce the oven to 300°F. Combine all the ingredients in a food processor. Purée until smooth and pour into the graham cracker crust. Place the pan inside a larger pan in the oven. Fill the larger pan with hot water. Bake for 1½ hours, then turn off the oven and allow the cheesecake to cool for 1 hour. When it is completely cooked, wrap well and refrigerate.

3. TO MAKE THE CARAMEL SAUCE: Combine the sugar and water in a large heavy saucepan over medium heat. Cook, swirling the pot around until the mixture is a deep caramel color and looks like syrup, about 8 minutes. Carefully pour in the cream (it will bubble up) and continue to cook for another minute. Cool to room temperature. Pour over the cheesecake before serving.

NOTE: *The caramel sauce can be made up to 2 weeks ahead and can be stored, covered, in the refrigerator.*

Buttermilk Panna Cotta with Fresh Spring Berries

❧

8 SERVINGS

1 tablespoon lemon juice
1 1/3 cups granulated sugar
1/4 cup hot water
4 cups heavy cream
2 cups buttermilk
2 packages unflavored gelatin powder
2 teaspoons vanilla extract
4 cups mixed fresh berries

1. In a small heavy saucepan, combine the lemon juice and 1/3 cup sugar. Cook over high heat, swirling occasionally, until the sugar caramelizes. Remove from the heat and carefully stir in the hot water. Pour the mixture evenly over the bottom of a 2-quart ring mold.

2. In a saucepan, combine the heavy cream and remaining 1 cup sugar and heat until the sugar dissolves.

3. In another saucepan, place the buttermilk and sprinkle the gelatin powder over it. Let it sit for 5 minutes to soften. Gently heat until the gelatin dissolves.

4. Combine the cream and buttermilk mixtures and add the vanilla extract. Pour into the prepared ring mold and refrigerate overnight.

5. Remove from the mold onto a serving platter and garnish with the fresh berries.

Chocolate Carrot Cake with White Chocolate Cream Cheese Frosting

12 SERVINGS

FOR THE CAKE:

8 eggs
3 3/4 cups sugar
1 1/2 cups vegetable oil
1 teaspoon salt
2 cups flour
1 cup unsweetened cocoa powder
1 1/2 teaspoon baking soda
1/2 teaspoon baking powder
4 cups grated carrots

FOR THE FROSTING:

1 cup butter
1 pound powdered sugar
2 cups cream cheese
2 teaspoons vanilla extract
1 pound white chocolate, melted
   and cooled

1. TO MAKE THE CAKE: Preheat the oven to 350°F. In a standing mixer, beat the eggs and sugar on high speed until the mixture is pale yellow and tripled in volume. Gradually add the oil with the mixer running.

2. Sift together the dry ingredients and stir into the egg mixture. Fold in the carrots. Pour into two 10-inch cake pans. Bake for 1 hour, or until a cake tester inserted into the middle comes out clean.

3. TO MAKE THE FROSTING: Cream the butter and sugar in a medium bowl. Add the cream cheese a little at a time. Mix in the vanilla and white chocolate.

4. Frost the cake after it has cooled.

Amore Baci Caffè (Love and Kisses Coffee)

1 SERVING

1 1/2 ounces crème de cacao (dark, chocolate bean flavored liqueur)
1 1/2 ounces Frangelico (toasted hazelnut liqueur)
5 ounces espresso
1 dollop of chocolate whipped cream* (made from 1 cup cream and 2 tablespoons chocolate sauce)

Pour the liqueurs into a coffee cup, fill with espresso, and top with chocolate whipped cream.

*NOTE: To make chocolate whipped cream, whip 2 tablespoons chocolate sauce in with 1 cup whipping cream.

zuppa de pesce, 156
see also specific fish and shellfish
fondue, chocolate, 220
fritters, pumpkin ricotta, 234
fudge, spiced pumpkin, 230
fusilli with roasted tomatoes, seasonal
   mushrooms, spinach, garlic, and
   extra-virgin olive oil, 97

garganelli with rock shrimp, zucchini,
   and toasted bread crumbs, 107
gnocchi, pumpkin, with grated amaretti
   cookies, 110

herbal salad with fresh parsley, tarragon,
   chive, Peekytoe crab, and edible
   flowers, 68

ice cream pie, chocolate Oreo, 239

kabobs, vegetable, with zucchini,
   peppers, yellow squash, and
   eggplant, 203
kiwi lime tart, 241

lamb:
   herb-crusted baby rack of, 169
   marinated and grilled Sicilian leg of
     lamb steaks, 184
   pot roast with creamy polenta, 182
lasagna:
   cheese, 99
   meatball, 104–5
lemon zucchini bread, 214
lentil soup, 55
lobster, grilled, and summer sweet corn,
   145

maple zucchini bread, 214
mascarpone cheese pistachio, tort,
   228–29
meatball lasagna, 104
meats and poultry, 159–90
   bollito misto con salsa verde (mixed
     boiled meat with green sauce), 167
   see also specific meats and poultry
menus, special holiday, 25–35
mushrooms:
   and grilled sea scallops wrapped
     with pancetta, lemon, and fresh
     herbs, 139
   wild, and chickpea soup with
     spareribs, 58
mussels, steamed Maine, and Manila
   clams, 137

Napoleon, heart-shaped banana
   caramel, 237

onions, red, and watermelon salad with
   watercress and Muscat vinaigrette,
   73
orange(s):
   blood, panna cotta, 238
   blossom pound cake, 234
oysters, fried, for salad, 71

panettone:
   bread pudding, 231
   toasted, with spiced mascarpone and
     orange supremes, 241
panna cotta:
   blood orange, 238
   buttermilk, with fresh spring
     berries, 245
panzenella skewers with mozzarella,
   tomato, and focaccia bread, 50
pappardelle with duck ragu, 93
pasta, 81–109
   al forno with tomatoes and basil,
     106
   cheese lasagna, 99
   e fagioli, 103
   meatball lasagna, 104–5
   salad, cold farro, with grilled
     vegetables, mozzarella, Pecorino
     cheese, and herb vinaigrette, 76
   with zucchini Calabrian-style with
     caramelized onions, lemon zest,
     and bread crumbs, 90
   see also specific pastas
peach upside down cake, 233
pears and apple crisp with almond
   crumb topping, 223
penne:
   with fresh tomato sauce, 100
   gratin, 94
   with veal and chicken Bolognese, 96
   whole wheat, with braised beets,
     Gorgonzola cheese, and walnuts,
     86
peppers, red, and tomatoes, marinated
   grilled, with olives and anchovies,
   202
pesto sauce, string beans, Yukon Gold
   potatoes, and marigold petals,
   fettuccine with, 109
pie:
   chocolate Oreo ice cream, 239
   eggplant and zucchini, 123
pistachio mascarpone tort, 228–29

pizza Margherita, grilled, 43–44
polenta, creamy:
   with chicken liver ragu, pancetta,
     caramelized onions, and wild
     mushrooms, 54
   with mascarpone cheese, 199
   with wild spring mushrooms,
     fontina, and mozzarella, 120–21
pork:
   chops, prosciutto-wrapped, 169
   Italian dry-rub BBQ ribs, 190
   loin, roast, maple- and bourbon-
     glazed, stuffed with apples and
     sun-dried cranberries, 185
   shoulder, braised, with tomato,
     fennel, onion, and Barolo wine,
     177–78
   spareribs, wild mushroom and
     chickpea soup with, 58
potato(es):
   grilled fingerling, with Gorgonzola
     cheese, 204
   salad, Sicilian, 196
   and zucchini chips with Gorgonzola
     cheese, 55
pots de crème, lavender, 218
pudding:
   bittersweet chocolate, 220
   cake, bittersweet chocolate, with
     vanilla gelato, 215
   rice, Arborio, 217
pumpkin:
   baked, stuffed with sausage, rice, and
     mozzarella, 174
   fudge, spiced, 230
   gnocchi with grated amaretti
     cookies, 110
   ricotta fritters, 234
   roasted, and beetroot salad with goat
     cheese and toasted pumpkin
     seeds, 79
   sweet potato-stuffed, 124

rice:
   balls, Italian, 49
   pudding, Arborio, 217
   and sausage turkey stuffing, 205
ricotta cheese pumpkin fritters, 234
risotto, 111–14

salads, 63–79
salmon:
   baked, wrapped in zucchini, 157
   cartoccio, 154
   grilled, cured with dried chamomile